T0268564

CAMBRIDGE
UNIVERSITY PRESS

Physics

for Cambridge IGCSE™

PRACTICAL WORKBOOK

Gillian Nightingale

CAMBRIDGE
UNIVERSITY PRESS

University Printing House, Cambridge CB2 8BS, United Kingdom

One Liberty Plaza, 20th Floor, New York, NY 10006, USA

477 Williamstown Road, Port Melbourne, VIC 3207, Australia

314–321, 3rd Floor, Plot 3, Splendor Forum, Jasola District Centre, New Delhi – 110025, India

103 Penang Road, #05 -06/07, Visioncrest Commercial, Singapore 238467

Cambridge University Press is part of the University of Cambridge.

It furthers the University's mission by disseminating knowledge in the pursuit of
education, learning and research at the highest international levels of excellence.

www.cambridge.org
Information on this title: www.cambridge.org/9781108744539

Second edition 2016
Third edition 2021

20 19 18 17 16 15 14 13 12 11 10 9 8 7 6 5

Printed in Malaysia by Vivar Printing

A catalogue record for this publication is available from the British Library

ISBN 978-1-108-74453-9 Practical Workbook Paperback with Digital Access (2 Years)

Additional resources for this publication at www.cambridge.org/go

Illustrations by Tech-Set Ltd.

DEDICATED TEACHER AWARDS

Teachers play an important part in shaping futures. Our Dedicated Teacher Awards recognise the hard work that teachers put in every day.

Thank you to everyone who nominated this year; we have been inspired and moved by all of your stories. Well done to all of our nominees for your dedication to learning and for inspiring the next generation of thinkers, leaders and innovators.

Congratulations to our incredible winner and finalists!

WINNER

Patricia Abril	Stanley Manaay	Tiffany Cavanagh	Helen Comerford	John Nicko Coyoca	Meera Rangarajan
New Cambridge School, Colombia	Salvacion National High School, Philippines	Trident College Solwezi, Zambia	Lumen Christi Catholic College, Australia	University of San Jose-Recoletos, Philippines	RBK International Academy, India

For more information about our dedicated teachers and their stories, go to
dedicatedteacher.cambridge.org

CAMBRIDGE
UNIVERSITY PRESS

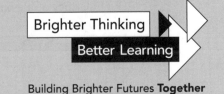

Brighter Thinking
Better Learning

Building Brighter Futures **Together**

> Contents

❯ How to use this series

We offer a comprehensive, flexible array of resources for the Cambridge IGCSE™ Physics syllabus. We provide targeted support and practice for the specific challenges we've heard that students face: learning science with English as a second language; learners who find the mathematical content within science difficult; and developing practical skills.

The coursebook provides coverage of the full Cambridge IGCSE Physics syllabus. Each chapter explains facts and concepts, and uses relevant real-world examples of scientific principles to bring the subject to life. Together with a focus on practical work and plenty of active learning opportunities, the coursebook prepares learners for all aspects of their scientific study. At the end of each chapter, examination-style questions offer practice opportunities for learners to apply their learning.

The digital teacher's resource contains detailed guidance for all topics of the syllabus, including common misconceptions identifying areas where learners might need extra support, as well as an engaging bank of lesson ideas for each syllabus topic. Differentiation is emphasised with advice for identification of different learner needs and suggestions of appropriate interventions to support and stretch learners. The teacher's resource also contains support for preparing and carrying out all the investigations in the practical workbook, including a set of sample results for when practicals aren't possible.

The teacher's resource also contains scaffolded worksheets and unit tests for each chapter. Answers for all components are accessible to teachers for free on the Cambridge GO platform.

The skills-focused workbook has been carefully constructed to help learners develop the skills that they need as they progress through their Cambridge IGCSE Physics course, providing further practice of all the topics in the coursebook. A three-tier, scaffolded approach to skills development enables students to gradually progress through 'focus', 'practice' and 'challenge' exercises, ensuring that every learner is supported. The workbook enables independent learning and is ideal for use in class or as homework.

The Cambridge IGCSE Physics practical workbook provides learners with additional opportunities for hands-on practical work, giving them full guidance and support that will help them to develop their investigative skills. These skills include planning investigations, selecting and handling apparatus, creating hypotheses, recording and displaying results, and analysing and evaluating data.

Mathematics is an integral part of scientific study, and one that learners often find a barrier to progression in science. The Maths Skills for Cambridge IGCSE Physics write-in workbook has been written in collaboration with the Association for Science Education, with each chapter focusing on several maths skills that students need to succeed in their Physics course.

Our research shows that English language skills are the single biggest barrier to students accessing international science. This write-in workbook contains exercises set within the context of Cambridge IGCSE Physics topics to consolidate understanding and embed practice in aspects of language central to the subject. Activities range from practising using comparative adjectives in the context of measuring density, to writing a set of instructions using the imperative for an experiment investigating frequency and pitch.

> How to use this book

Throughout this book, you will notice lots of different features that will help your learning. These are explained below. Answers are accessible for free for teachers in the supporting resources section of Cambridge GO.

INTRODUCTION

These set the scene for each chapter and indicate the important concepts. These start with the sentence 'The investigations in this chapter will...'

KEY WORDS

Key vocabulary and definitions are given at the start of each investigation. You will also find definitions of these words in the Glossary at the back of this book.

COMMAND WORDS

Command words that appear in the syllabus are highlighted in the exam-style questions and the Cambridge International definition is given. You will also find these definitions in the Glossary at the back of the book.

LEARNING INTENTIONS

- These set out the learning intentions for each investigation.

> In the learning intentions table, Supplement content is indicated with a large arrow and a darker background, as in the example here.

The investigations include information on **equipment**, **safety considerations** and **method**. They also include **questions** to test your understanding on recording data, handling data, analysis and evaluation.

Remember that there is a **Safety section** at the start of this book – you should refer to this often, as it contains general advice that is applicable to many of the investigations.

REFLECTION

These encourage you to reflect on your learning approaches.

TIPS

The information in these boxes will help you complete the questions, and give you support in areas that you might find difficult.

Supplement content

Where content is intended for learners who are studying the Supplement content of the syllabus as well as the Core, this is indicated in the main text using the arrow and the bar, as on the left here.

EXAM-STYLE QUESTIONS

More demanding exam-style questions can be found at the end of each chapter, some of which may require use of knowledge from previous chapters. The answers to these questions are accessible to teachers for free on the Cambridge GO site.

Note for teachers

The teacher's resource in this series includes sample data and support notes for each of the practical investigations in this practical workbook. You can find information about planning and setting up each investigation, further safety guidance, common errors to be aware of, differentiation ideas and additional areas for discussion.

Answers to all questions in this practical workbook are accessible to teachers at www.cambridge.org/go

> Introduction

Investigations in and out of the laboratory have been at the forefront of physics discoveries for most of the last two centuries. The Cavendish Laboratory, at Cambridge University in England, has seen some of the most remarkable and pioneering discoveries since it was established in the 19th century. J.J. Thomson discovered the electron and Ernest Rutherford was able to recreate fission. Their experimental methods and consequent discoveries revolutionised physicists' views on the world. Without practical experimentation, none of these discoveries would have been possible.

Practical skills form the foundation of any physics course. We hope that by using this book, you will gain confidence in this exciting and essential area of study. This book has been written to prepare Cambridge IGCSE Physics learners for their practical and alternatives to practical examinations for Cambridge IGCSE Physics and IGCSE (9–1) (0625/0972). For either paper, you need to be able to demonstrate a wide range of practical skills. Through the investigations and questions in this book you can build and refine your abilities so that you gain enthusiasm in tackling laboratory work. These interesting and enjoyable investigations are also intended to inspire enthusiasm for practical physics. We have taken care to ensure that this book contains work that is safe and accessible for you to complete. Before attempting any of these activities, though, make sure that you have read the safety section and are following the safety regulations of the place where you study.

Answers to the exercises in this practical workbook can be found in the Teacher's resource. Ask your teacher to provide access to the answers.

Safety

Despite the fact that Bunsen burners, electrical circuits and chemicals are used on a regular basis, the science laboratory is one of the safest classrooms in a school. This is due to the emphasis on safety and the focus on following precautions and procedures resulting from regular risk assessment.

It is important that you follow the safety rules set out by your teacher. Your teacher will know the names of materials, and the hazards associated with them, as part of their risk assessment for performing the investigations. They will share this information with you as part of their safety brief or demonstration of the investigation.

You should follow the guidance and the safety precautions in each of the investigations in this book. You should aim to use the safety rules as additional direction to help in planning your own investigations.

Here are some precautions that will help to ensure your safety when carrying out most investigations in this workbook.

- Wear safety spectacles to protect your eyes.
- Tie back hair and any loose items of clothing.
- Tidy away personal belongings to avoid tripping over them.
- Wear gloves and protective clothing, as described in the book or by your teacher.
- Turn the Bunsen burner to the cool, yellow flame when it is not in use.
- Keep all electrical circuits away from water.
- Observe hazard symbols and chemical information provided with all substances and solutions.

Many of the investigations require teamwork or group work. It is the responsibility of your group to make sure that you plan how to be safe as carefully as you plan the rest of the investigation.

> Practical skills and support

The Experimental Skills and investigations outlined in the Cambridge Assessment International Education IGCSE Physics syllabus focus on skills and abilities you need to develop to work as a scientist. Each of these aspects have been broken down for you below with a reference to the chapters in this title that cover it. This will enable you to identify where you have practised each skill.

Skills grid

Chapter	1	2	3	4	5	6	7	8	9	10	11	12	13	14	15	16	17	18	19	20	21	22	23	24	25
Experimental skills and investigations																									
1.1 demonstrate knowledge of how to safely use techniques																									
1.2 demonstrate knowledge of how to use apparatus and materials																									
1.3 demonstrate knowledge of how to follow a sequence of instructions																									
2. plan experiments and investigations																									
3.1 make and record observations																									
3.2 make and record measurements																									
3.3 make and record estimates																									
4.1 interpret experimental observations and data																									
4.2 evaluate experimental observations and data																									
5.1 evaluate methods																									
5.2 suggest possible improvements to methods																									
Constructing own table																									
Drawing/analysing a graph																									
Planning safety of an investigation																									
Mathematical calculations																									

Apparatus

You will need to be able to identify, use and draw a variety of scientific apparatus. Complete the table below by adding the diagrams and uses for each piece of apparatus.

Apparatus	Diagram	Uses
timer		
balance/scales		
beaker		
Bunsen burner		
tripod		
test-tube		

Measuring

Being able to take accurate measurements is an essential skill for all physics students. As part of your Cambridge IGCSE Physics course you will be expected to be able to take accurate measurements using a variety of different apparatus. When using measuring cylinders you will need to look for the meniscus which is the bottom of the curve formed by the liquid.

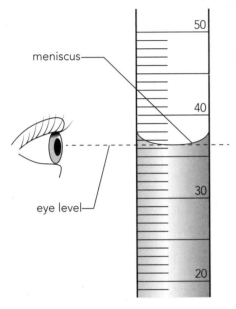

Thermometers are a very common tool for measuring temperature in physics experiments so you will need to be able to take readings reliably. Not all of the points of the scale on a thermometer will be marked but you will still need to be able to determine the temperature. To do this you will need to work out the value of each graduation. In the diagram below there are four marks between 95 and 100. Each of these marks indicates 1°C.

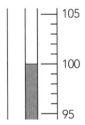

Recording

When working on investigations the ability to record data accurately is very important. Sometimes a table will be supplied; however, you need to be able to draw your own table with the correct headings and units.

The first task is to identify the independent and dependent variables for the investigation you are doing. The independent variable is the one which you are changing to see if this affects the dependent variable. The dependent variable is the one which you will measure and record the results of in the table. The names of these two variables and their units need to go into the top two boxes in you results table. The independent variable goes in the left hand box and the dependent variable goes in the right hand box. Separate the name of the variables and units using a forward slash / e.g. time/ seconds. Remember that the column headings need to be physical quantities (time, mass, temperature etc.)

Next count how many different values you have for the independent variable. This is how many rows you will need to add below the column headings. Finally add the values for the independent variable into the left hand column. Your table is now ready for you to add the results from your investigation in the right hand column.

Independent variable / units	Dependent variable / units

Drawing graphs

When drawing a graph it is useful to follow a set procedure every time to ensure that when you are finished the graph is complete.

Axes

You must label the axes with your independent and dependent variables. The independent variable is used to label the x-axis (horizontal axis) and the dependent variable is used to label the y-axis (vertical axis). Remember to also add the units for each of the variables. An easy way to ensure that you get this correct is to copy the column headings from the table of data you are using to draw the graph.

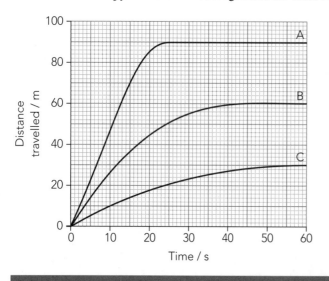
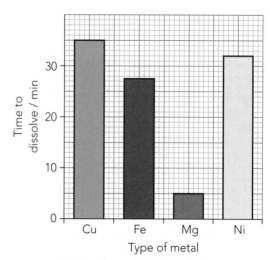

TIP

At the top of any table of data you have to use, write the letters X and Y next to the independent and dependent variable to remind you which axis each goes on.

The second stage of drawing a graph is adding a scale. You must select a scale that allows you to use more than half of the graph grid in both directions. Choose a sensible ratio to allow you to easily plot your points (e.g. each 1 cm on the graph grid represents 1, 2, 5, 10, 50 or 100 units of the variable). If you choose to use other numbers for your scale it becomes much more difficult to plot your graph.

Now you are ready to plot the points of data on the graph grid. You can use either crosses (x) or a point enclosed inside a circle to plot your points, but take your time to make sure these are plotted accurately. Remember to use a sharp pencil as large dots make it difficult to see the place the point is plotted and may make it difficult for the accuracy of the plot to be decided.

Finally, a best-fit line needs to be added. This must be a single thin line or smooth curve. It does not need to go through all of the points but it should have roughly half the number of points on each side if the data is scattered. Remember to ignore any anomalous data when you draw your line of best fit. Some good examples of lines of best fit that you should use are shown below:

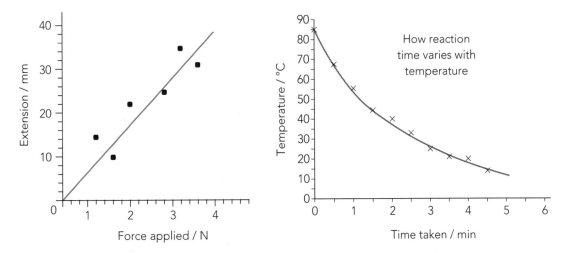

Variables

The independent and dependent variables have already been discussed but there is a third type of variable that you will need to be familiar with: controlled variables. These are variables that are kept the same during an investigation to make sure that they do not affect the results. If these variables are not kept the same then we cannot be sure that it is our independent variable having an effect on the results.

Example

Two students are investigating how changing the temperature affects the rate that gas is produced when adding magnesium to an acid. They do not control the volume of acid of the mass of magnesium used each time. This means that there is no pattern in their results, as if they use more acid magnesium more gas is produced regardless of the temperature used.

Reliability, accuracy and precision

A common task in this book will be to suggest how to improve the method used in an investigation to improve its reliability/accuracy/precision. Before we come to how these improvements can be made, it is important that you have a solid understanding of what each of these words mean.

Reliability is about the likelihood of getting the same results if you did the investigation again and being sure that the results are not just down to chance. Reliability is now often called repeatability for this reason. Repeat measurements help to reduce percentage uncertainty caused by random errors or make the errors less significant. If you can repeat an investigation several times and get the same result each time it is said to be reliable.

The reliability can be improved by:

- Controlling other variables well so they do not affect the results
- Repeating the experiment until no anomalous results are achieved
- Increasing precision.

Precision is about having very little spread of results from the mean.

The precision can be improved by:

- Using apparatus that has smaller scale divisions.

Accuracy is a measure of how close the measured value is to the true value. The accuracy of the results depends on the measuring apparatus used and the skill of the person taking the measurements, which reduces systematic errors.

The accuracy can be improved by:

- Improving the design of an investigation to reduce errors
- Using more precise apparatus
- Repeating the measurement and calculating the mean.

However if your investigation includes systematic errors (errors which are present every time you do the investigation, such as measuring to the wrong point of a meniscus each time) then repeating the investigation will not improve the accuracy as the systematic error will be present in each measurement.

You can observe how these terms are used in the diagram below.

Reliability v Precision v Accuracy

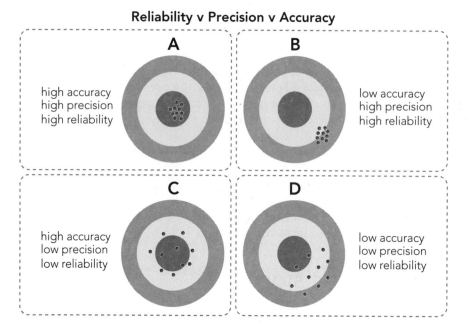

Designing an investigation

When asked to design an investigation, you must think carefully about what level of detail to include. You must identify what your independent variable is and which values you are planning to use for it. The dependent variable must also be identified along with how you are going to measure it. The next thing you need to do is to suggest how you will control other variables. Finally, outline the method in a series of numbered steps that is detailed enough for someone else to follow. Remember to include repeat readings to help improve reliability.

> Chapter 1
Making measurements

Practical investigation 1.1:
Estimating measurements

KEY WORDS

circumference: the distance around the outside of a circle

diameter: the length of a straight line that goes from one side of a circle to the other and passes through the centre of the circle

estimate: use information available to decide on a value that is appropriate

IN THIS INVESTIGATION YOU WILL:

- take accurate measurements of mass, time and distance using appropriate equipment

- calculate average values.

YOU WILL NEED:

- metre ruler • stopwatch • top-pan balance • newton scale
- 30 cm ruler (for analysis section)

Safety

- Before you start recording the time for star jumps, check that the surrounding area is clear of objects.

- Make sure the person performing star jumps is wearing footwear suitable for this task.

Getting started

Familiarise yourself with the names of the equipment and what they measure from the skills section at the start of this book. Fill in the table provided to show which piece of equipment you will use for each type of measurement.

Measurement	Equipment
length	
volume	
mass	
time	

Use this table to help you during your investigation.

Method

1   Look at everything you are going to measure. Estimate each value and record your estimates in the table that has been provided.

2   Take measurements of:

- the height of the person sitting next to you (in cm)

- how long it takes a student to perform ten star jumps

- the length, width and thickness of a glass block

- the diameter of a piece of wire

- the mass of a bag of sugar.

Take each measurement three times.

Recording data

1   Record your measurements in the table. Remember to include the appropriate units.

Measurement type	Estimated value	Measured value			Average measurement
		1	2	3	

> **TIP**
>
> Make sure you record all measurements to the same number of significant figures or decimal places.

Handling data

2   Review your table. Are all of the measurements to the same number of decimal places or significant figures? Correct any that are not.

3   Calculate the average value for each measurement. Write the average values in the table.

Analysis

4   Compare your estimated and measured values. Comment on the values. Make reference to the data in your table to support your comments.

....

....

5 Calculate the volume of the glass block, based on the measurements you have taken.

....

....

Evaluation

6 Were the measuring instruments that you chose suitable in each case? Explain your answer and suggest what other instruments you could have used.

....

....

7 List three of the instruments you used and give the precision of these instruments.

TIP
The precision of an instrument is the smallest scale division on the instrument.

....

....

....

Practical investigation 1.2: The simple pendulum

KEY WORDS
mean: the mathematical term for the average of a range of numbers
meniscus: the lowest point of the top of a liquid
oscillation: the movement of an object from its start point to its furthest point and back again to the start
time period: the time taken for one complete oscillation

KEY EQUATION
average: the average of 12, 15 and 16 is 14.3: $\dfrac{12 + 15 + 16}{3} = 14.3$

Safety

Clamp the stand to the bench to ensure it is stable and cannot fall over and cause injury.

Getting started

Take a pendulum. Hold it between your fingers and look at how the pendulum moves.

Think about the things that you will need to consider in order to time the oscillation of the pendulum accurately. Write them down here.

....

....

Now, working with a partner, think of ways in which you could adapt your method to make your measurements more accurate. Write them down here.

....

....

Method

1   Tie the string to the pendulum bob to make a pendulum.

2   Hang the pendulum from the clamp stand and wait for it to come to rest (stop moving).

3   Use the ruler to measure the length of the pendulum from where the pendulum is held to the centre of its bob (its centre of gravity).

4   Keeping the string straight, move the pendulum bob to one side and release it, allowing it to swing at a steady pace. Use the stopwatch to time ten complete oscillations.

5   Repeat twice more and take an average of the results.

6   Repeat for four different lengths of pendulum.

Recording data

1 Record your measurements in the table.

Length of pendulum / cm	Time taken for ten oscillations / s				Time period (time taken for one oscillation) / s
	1	2	3	Average (mean)	

Handling data

2 Calculate the time period for each pendulum length. Write the values in the table.

Analysis

3 Draw a graph of pendulum length against time period.

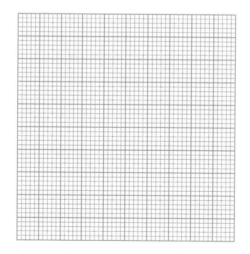

4 State and explain whether the length of the pendulum has an effect on the time period of an oscillation. Use your results to support your answer.

....

....

....

....

Evaluation

5   Suggest another variable that might affect the time period of an oscillation.

....

....

REFLECTION

How did you find recording the oscillations of your pendulum? With your partner, discuss one way in which you could have improved this investigation to make it easier to record the oscillations.

Practical investigation 1.3: Calculating the density of liquids

IN THIS INVESTIGATION YOU WILL:

- determine the densities of three common liquids by taking measurements of volume and mass.

YOU WILL NEED:

- $100\,cm^3$ measuring cylinder   • oil   • saltwater solution   • water   • balance
- safety goggles

Safety

- Some of the fluids in this investigation can cause mild irritation to the eyes. Use safety goggles at all times.

- Clear any spills immediately to prevent slipping.

Getting started

With your partner, discuss why knowing the density of a fluid is important. Write some ideas down in the space provided.

TIP
Think about convection and the weather.

....

....

....

....

When you measure the volume of a liquid, it is important to ensure that the reading is taken correctly. The reading should always be taken at eye level, and using the meniscus of the liquid. Look at the example in Figure 1.1 and then try to read the volume of the remaining three measuring cylinders.

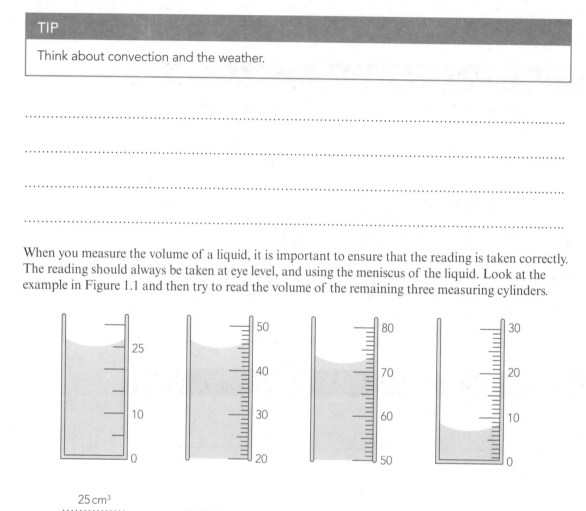

25 cm³
....

Figure 1.1: Taking a reading from a measuring cylinder.

Method

1 Place the measuring cylinder on the balance. Set the balance to zero.

2 Add 50 cm³ of water to the measuring cylinder. Record the volume and mass of the water in the table on the next page.

3 Repeat for 60 cm³, 70 cm³, 80 cm³, 90 cm³ and 100 cm³. Record the volume and mass of the water in the table on the next page.

4 Empty and dry the measuring cylinder. Repeat steps **1–3** for the saltwater solution and the oil.

Recording data

1 Record your measurements in the tables.

Water	
Volume / cm³	Mass / g

Saltwater solution	
Volume / cm³	Mass / g

Oil	
Volume / cm³	Mass / g

Handling data

2 Use your results to plot a graph of volume against mass for each of the liquids you have measured. Plot all three graphs on the grid provided.

> **TIP**
>
> When you draw the graph, label each axis and include the appropriate unit. For this graph, plot the volume along the horizontal axis and the mass up the vertical axis.
>
> Remember to choose an appropriate scale for each axis.

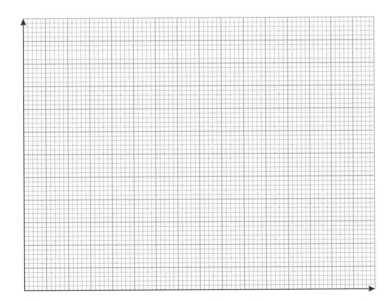

Analysis

3   Draw a line of best fit for each of the liquids you have tested. Label them clearly.

4   The gradient of the line of best fit in each graph is equal to the density of the liquid. By looking at your graph, predict which liquid has the highest density. In the space below, explain how you can make this assumption by sight alone.

....

....

....

5   Calculate the gradient of each of the lines of best fit. Do your values support your answer to question 4?

Water   ....

....

Oil   ....

....

Saltwater solution   ....

....

6   Liquids that are less dense float on top of more dense substances. The liquids do not mix. In the measuring beaker shown, draw in the order in which the liquids would settle, labelling each one clearly.

Evaluation

7   Your teacher will give you the actual values of density for the liquids you have tested.
How do your results compare? Suggest two reasons why your results may be different.

....

....

....

....

8   An oil spill occurs out at sea. A student suggests that a clean-up operation would be impossible
because the two substances would mix. Do you think the student is correct? Comment on the
student's statement, relating it to the experiment you have conducted here.

....

....

....

....

REFLECTION

In this investigation you had to calculate the gradient of your line of best fit. Discuss with
two other groups the values they calculated. How different were they compared to yours?
If you were a scientist trying to evaluate the density of a particular liquid, how would you
accommodate the differing results?

EXAM-STYLE QUESTIONS

1 A student has been asked to determine the material from which a key is made.

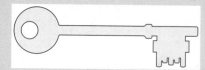

The student has been given a table which lists the densities of a variety of common metals based on measurements taken from $1\,cm^3$ metal blocks found in the laboratory.

Type of metal	Density / g/cm³
aluminium	2.7
iron	7.9
lead	11.4
steel	8.4

The student fills a displacement can with water and carefully adds the key, using a measuring cylinder to collect the water that is displaced. The displaced water collected in the measuring cylinder is displayed in the figure.

cm³

15
14
13
12
11
10
9
8
7
6
5
4
3
2
1

a **i** Show clearly on the diagram the line of sight you would use to obtain an accurate reading. [2]

ii **State** the volume of the key. [1]

....

COMMAND WORD

state: express in clear terms

b i The student then takes the key, dries it and uses a balance to measure its mass. The mass of the key is 65.01 g.
Calculate the density of the material from which the key is made, using the equation for density. [3]

....

....

ii Using the table of densities, **determine** the metal from which the key is most likely to be made. [1]

....

....

c The density of water is 1 g/cm³. Which of the metals in the table would you expect to float?

Explain your answer. [3]

....

....

[Total: 10]

2 A student has been asked to measure the average speed of a child's toy race car as it goes around a circular track.

a i The student uses the equation for average speed to determine that they need to measure the distance of the track and the time taken for the car to go around the track.

Suggest appropriate equipment for taking these measurements in the table provided. [2]

Quantity	Measuring device	Resolution
distance		
time taken		

ii State an appropriate resolution for each of these instruments in the final column of the table. [2]

CONTINUED

b i The diagram shows a scale drawing of the circular race track. Use the diagram to calculate the distance travelled by the car in one lap. [2]

Scale = 1 cm : 5 cm

....

....

ii The readings for the time taken by the student are given in the table.

Time taken / s	0.48	0.49	0.5

Suggest one way she could improve the tabulation of her data. [1]

....

....

iii Calculate the average time taken for one lap. [1]

....

....

iv Calculate the average speed for the car around the race track. Include the relevant units in your answer. [2]

....

....

c The student notices that the time taken for the car to go around the track is very short. She is worried that the measurements are not accurate enough. Suggest one way in which she could improve the accuracy. [2]

....

....

[Total: 12]

> Chapter 2

Describing motion

THE INVESTIGATIONS IN THIS CHAPTER WILL:

- allow you to understand and track changes in the movement of objects. This is useful for understanding performance in sport – for example, the performance of Formula 1® racing cars.

Practical investigation 2.1:
Average speed

KEY WORD

speed: how quickly an object travels over a specific distance

KEY EQUATION

$$\text{average speed} = \frac{\text{total distance travelled}}{\text{total time taken}}$$

IN THIS INVESTIGATION YOU WILL:

- take measurements of length and time and use them to plot a distance–time graph
- calculate the gradient of a distance–time graph to find the speed.

YOU WILL NEED:

- chalk or cones • measuring tape • stopwatches

Safety

- Check the area is clear of trip hazards.
- Make sure that the person who will be running is well warmed up and is wearing sensible shoes for running.

Getting started

In your group, consider the following:

- What could impact the accuracy of the times that you record?

- How will you try to ensure that your readings are accurate?

Method

1   Use the chalk to mark a starting point.

2   Use the measuring tape and chalk to measure and mark a distance of 20 m from this point. Then mark 40 m, 60 m, 80 m and 100 m from the starting point.

3   Choose a member of the group to be the starter. They will indicate to the timer when to start the stopwatch.

4   Choose a member of the group to run the 100 m. The other members of the group will act as timers. Each timer should take a stopwatch and stand at a different 20 m interval (20 m, 40 m, 60 m, 80 m, 100 m).

5   The timers start their stopwatches when the starter indicates that the runner starts to run, and stop their stopwatches when the runner passes their marker.

Recording data

1   Use the table to record the times taken to run 20 m, 40 m, 60 m, 80 m and 100 m.

Distance / m	Time / s
0	
20	
40	
60	
80	
100	

Handling data

2 Use the data from your table to plot a distance–time graph of your results on the grid provided. Plot distance on the vertical axis and time along the horizontal axis. Remember to label your axes and include the relevant units.

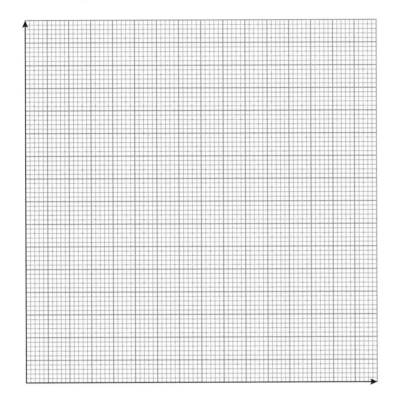

Analysis

3 Without doing any calculation, state which section of the run was the fastest. Give reasons for your answer.

....

....

4 Calculate the speed during the slowest and fastest sections of the run.

....

....

....

....

5   The overall gradient of this distance–time graph represents the average speed for the whole journey. How could you measure the speed at the 50 m point?

....

....

....

6   The gradient of a distance–time graph represents the speed of the travelling object. Use your graph to calculate the average speed across the whole 100 m. Show how you have done this, clearly, on the graph.

....

....

Evaluation

7   State the precision of the measuring instruments you used and suggest one way in which you could improve the precision of your measurements.

....

8   When conducting this investigation, how did you ensure that all timers started their stopwatches at the same time?

....

....

....

9   How would the distance–time graph have differed if the runner accelerated gradually through the run?

....

....

REFLECTION

- In this investigation, it can be difficult to see the starter letting the runner go. With a friend discuss a few ways in which you could have improved the timers' ability to see the starter begin the experiment. Which of your suggestions would be the most accurate?

- Stopping the stopwatch at the correct instant can also prove a challenge. Discuss the way in which you reduced error here. What others ways could you have reduced this error?

Practical investigation 2.2: Speed–time graphs using ticker tape

KEY WORDS

acceleration: the rate at which the speed of an object changes

light gate: detects the length of time a light beam is broken for, when used in conjunction with a data logger

KEY EQUATION

$$\text{acceleration} = \frac{\text{change in velocity}}{\text{time}}$$

IN THIS INVESTIGATION YOU WILL:

- plot a speed–time graph
- calculate the gradient of a speed–time graph, and therefore the acceleration.
- calculate the area under a speed–time graph, and therefore the distance travelled.

YOU WILL NEED:

- trolley • ticker timer • ticker tape • power pack • ramp • plain-coloured paper
- scissors • glue • sticky tape • block to support ramp

Safety

- The ramps are long and heavy so work in pairs to carry them, to avoid injury.
- Place a buffer at the end of the ramp to catch the trolley, to prevent injury to feet or damage to the trolley or floor.

Getting started

The frequency of the ticker timer is 50 Hz. This means that it creates a dot 50 times in 1 second. Calculate the time between one dot and the next.

....

....

If you have ten spaces between dots on your strip of paper (11 dots), what time period does this represent?

....

....

Use these calculations to help you calculate the time represented by each of your strips in the investigation.

Method

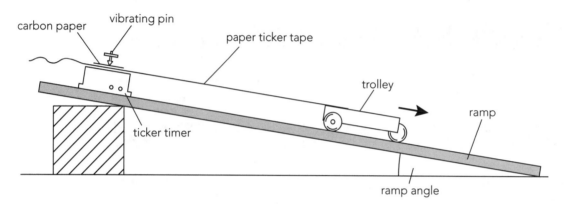

Figure 2.1: Ticker tape experiment apparatus.

1   Set up the apparatus as shown in Figure 2.1, ensuring the ticker tape goes underneath the carbon paper disc in the ticker timer.

2   Fasten the ticker tape securely to the trolley. Keep the trolley stationary and turn on the ticker timer.

3   Release the trolley down the ramp and catch it at the bottom. Cut the ticker tape at the timer.

4   Find the start on the ticker tape. From the first dot, count ten gaps. Cut the tape on the 11th dot.

5   Repeat until all of the tape is cut into sections of ten. Label the sections of tape in the order in which you cut them.

Handling data

1   You have cut the ticker tape at every tenth dot. Each section of ticker tape represents 0.2 seconds in time. The length of the tape is how far the trolley travelled in that time. This means that each piece of ticker tape represents the speed of the trolley in that time.

2   Draw the speed–time axes on a piece of plain paper. Speed is on the vertical axis, with a scale of 1 cm to represent a speed of 5 cm/s. Label the horizontal axis as time, in seconds, with 0.2 seconds divisions.

3   Glue the pieces of ticker tape vertically onto the graph, side by side, in the order that you cut them, with section 1 first, and with the long edges touching.

Analysis

4 From your graph, read the greatest speed of the trolley on its journey. Write it down.

....

5 Describe the shape of your graph. What does this tell you about the speed of the trolley during its journey?

....

....

....

....

6 Draw in a line of best fit. This should be a straight line that goes through the middle of the top dot on as many ticker tape pieces as possible.

7 Calculate the gradient of this line. What does this line represent?

....

....

....

....

8 The area under a speed–time graph is representative of the distance travelled. Calculate the distance travelled by the trolley from your graph.

....

....

....

Evaluation

9 It can sometimes be difficult to count the gaps in the ticker tape. State one way you overcame this difficulty.

....

....

10 Another student completes the same investigation, but their graph of results gives ticker tape strips of similar lengths. Suggest why this might have happened, and one way in which you could prevent this from happening.

....

....

....

....

11 Consider why a graph like this might be useful for a Formula 1® race car team. Write your ideas in the space below.

....

....

....

EXAM-STYLE QUESTIONS

1 A student is asked to use a light gate and interrupt card to investigate the speed of a trolley down a ramp. The student measures the speed of the trolley at different points along its journey down the path by moving the light gate to the positions marked on the diagram. The computer records the speed, v, and the time, t, taken.

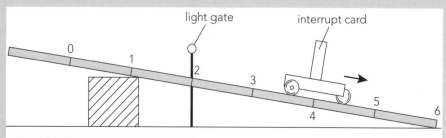

The student's results are shown in the table.

Light gate position	$\dfrac{v}{m/s}$	t / s
1	0.79	0.60
2	1.12	0.90
3	1.38	1.09
4	1.58	1.26
5	1.78	1.40
6	1.95	1.55

CONTINUED

a   Plot a graph of speed v/m/s (on the vertical axis) against time t/s
(on the horizontal axis). **[5]**

b   The gradient of the line represents the acceleration of the trolley.
Calculate the acceleration of the trolley and state its units. **[3]**

....

....

....

Units ....

c   Light gate position 6 was at the end of the ramp. Calculate the length
of the ramp. **[3]**

....

....

....

d   The student suggests that the acceleration is not uniform. **State** whether
or not this is correct. **Give** a reason to support your answer. **[2]**

Is this correct? ....

....

Reason ....

....

....

[Total: 13]

> Chapter 3

Forces and motion

Practical investigation 3.1:
Estimating the acceleration of free fall

KEY EQUATIONS

acceleration of free fall $= g = \dfrac{W}{m}$

Weight $=$ mass $\times g$

IN THIS INVESTIGATION YOU WILL:

- estimate the acceleration of free fall using the equation $g = w/m$.

YOU WILL NEED:

- force meter • variety of objects • top-pan balance

Getting started

At sea level, the accepted value for the acceleration of free fall is 9.81 m/s², which is often rounded to 10 m/s² to make calculations easier.

Suggest one reason why the value of the acceleration of free fall may change depending on your position on the Earth.

....

The acceleration of free fall is different depending on which planet you are on in the Solar System. Research the acceleration of free fall on three different planets and calculate what the weight of a 75 kg person would be on each of these planets using the equation for weight:

$$\text{weight} = \text{mass} \times g$$

....

....

....

Method

1   Select an object. Measure the mass of the object using the top-pan balance.

2   Measure the weight of the same object on the force meter.

3   Record your results in the table given in the Recording data section.

4   Repeat steps **1–3** for at least five more objects.

Recording data

1   Record your results in the table.

Object	Mass / kg	Weight / N

Handling data

2 Plot a graph of weight against mass with weight on the *y*-axis and mass on the *x*-axis.

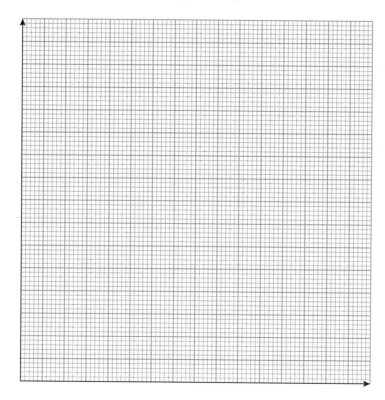

Analysis

3 Draw in a line of best fit for the points on your graph.

4 Looking at the equation for the acceleration of free fall, which can also be known as the gravitational field strength equation, the gradient of your line is equal to the acceleration of free fall:

$$g = \frac{W}{m}$$

Calculate the gradient of your line.

....

....

....

....

5   The accepted value for the acceleration of free fall is in the region of 9.8 m/s². How does your result compare with this? Give justification for why you think it might differ.

....

....

....

....

6   'The acceleration of free fall near the surface of the Earth is constant.' Do you agree with this statement? Use your graph to support your answer.

....

....

....

....

Evaluation

7   The experimental method you have used is not very accurate. Accuracy can be improved by increasing the resolution (i.e. the smallest division) of your instruments. State the resolution of your instruments used.

....

....

....

....

REFLECTION

Look at the method you used for this investigation. Discuss with your group how you could have improved this method to achieve more accurate results. Write your ideas below.

....

....

....

Practical investigation 3.2: Investigating the relationship between force, mass and acceleration

---
KEY WORD

variable: a quantity that can change

IN THIS INVESTIGATION YOU WILL:

- investigate the relationships between force and acceleration and mass and acceleration.

YOU WILL NEED:

- trolley of known mass • runway • three elastic bands • two pins • stopwatch
- masses up to 1 kg • adhesive putty • metre ruler • safety goggles

---

Safety

- Never try to carry runw rself. They should be carried by at least two people, to reduce the risk of injury.

- Place elastic bands on the pins securely and wear safety goggles to protect eyes.

Getting started

It is always good to consider how you will ensure that the measurements you will take will be accurate. In the table, write down how you will ensure that the following situations remain constant.

Situation	How will you prevent it?
Starting point of the trolley changing	
End point of the trolley changing	
Recording the time incorrectly	
Trolley colliding with the side of the runway	

Method

Increasing the force

1   At one end of the runway, insert the two pins either side of the runway and stretch one elastic band between them. Measure 1 m from the elastic band and mark a finish line on the runway.

2   Place the trolley on the runway, pull the elastic band and trolley back together by 3 cm and release, then record the time it takes the trolley to reach the finish line.

3   Add another elastic band to the pins and repeat step **2**.

4   Repeat for different numbers of elastic bands.

Increasing the mass

1   Use the equipment set up as above.

2   Place the trolley on the runway, pull the elastic band and trolley back together by 3 cm and release, then record the time it takes the trolley to reach the finish line.

3   Use adhesive putty to attach a mass to the trolley. Repeat step **2**.

4   Repeat with different masses attached to the trolley.

Recording data

Increasing the force

1   Record your results in this table.

Number of elastic bands	Time taken / s

Increasing the mass

2   Record your results in this table.

Mass of the trolley / kg	Time taken / s

Analysis

3 Write a conclusion about the relationship between the force acting on the trolley and its acceleration. Use your results to help justify your answer.

....

....

....

4 Write a conclusion about the relationship between the mass of the trolley and its acceleration. Use your results to help justify your answer.

....

....

....

Evaluation

5 Each of these investigations had control variables. These are variables that need to be kept constant so that they do not affect the outcome of the experiment. Suggest one control variable for each investigation.

Force investigation ....

Mass investigation ....

6 The reliability of results depends on how repeatable the results in the investigation are. Suggest one way in which you could prove that your results are reliable.

....

....

Practical investigation 3.3: Momentum in explosions

KEY WORDS

buffered: a way to reduce the impact or force

data logger: an electronic device that records information over a set period of time

KEY EQUATION

momentum = $p = mv$

IN THIS INVESTIGATION YOU WILL:

> apply the principle of conservation of momentum to an explosion between two trolleys.

YOU WILL NEED:

- metre ruler • trolleys • balance • two data loggers • interrupt cards • light gates
- small hammer • 1 kg masses • clamp stands and bosses

Safety

- If conducting the investigation on a bench, ensure the trolleys are buffered at either end to prevent damage to the trolleys or the floor and injury to feet.

- Take care to reduce risk of injury to hands and fingers when hitting the vertical rod in the trolley.

Getting started

It is important that when you record your data in a table, all values are recorded to the same number of significant figures (s.f.). Significant figures are those that tell you how large the number is, giving you an approximation to the required value. For example, 72 345 to 2 s.f. gives a value of 72 000 and 345 to 2 s.f. gives a value of 350. Using these examples, round the following values to 2 s.f.

Value	Value rounded to 2 s.f.
25 478	
679	
1.23	
0.056 78	
0.000 657 4	

Method

1   Measure a length of 5 m across the floor or a bench.

2   Measure the mass of two trolleys on the balance and record your results.

3   In the centre of the 5 m length, place the two trolleys back to back. Set up data loggers at either end of the 5 m space (2.5 m away from the back of each trolley, see Figure 3.1).

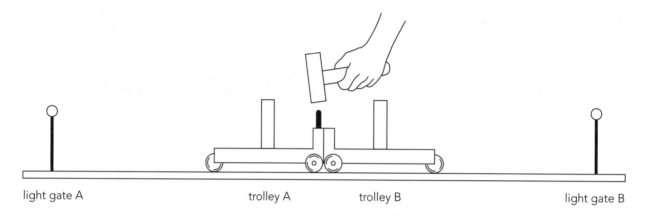

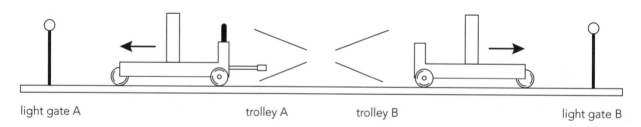

Figure 3.1: Experimental set-up for investigating momentum in explosions.

4   Set up the data logger to measure the velocity of each trolley as it passes through the light gate.

5   Hit the vertical release rod and record the velocity of each trolley as it passes through the light gate.

6   Repeat steps **2–5**, adding different masses to one trolley.

Recording data

1 Record your results in the table. Remember, when recording the velocity of the trolleys you must include a direction. Take trolley A's direction as positive and trolley B's direction as negative.

Mass of trolley A / kg	Velocity of trolley A / m/s	Momentum of trolley A / kg m/s	Mass of trolley B / kg	Velocity of trolley B / m/s	Momentum of trolley B / kg m/s

> **TIP**
>
> Remember to record all of your results to 2 significant figures.

Handling data

2 Calculate the momentum of the trolleys for each velocity, using the momentum equation, $p = mv$, and include this in your table.

Analysis

3 State why a direction is required for the velocity and therefore the momentum of the trolleys.

....

....

....

4 Compare the momentum of trolley A and trolley B. What conclusion can you make from this data? Give a justification for your answer.

....

....

....

Evaluation

5 Other students would like to use this method. Suggest one change they should make to the experiment in order to ensure the reliability of the results.

....

....

....

EXAM-STYLE QUESTIONS

1 A student is asked to investigate the relationship between the force applied to an object and its acceleration. The student sets up the equipment as shown.

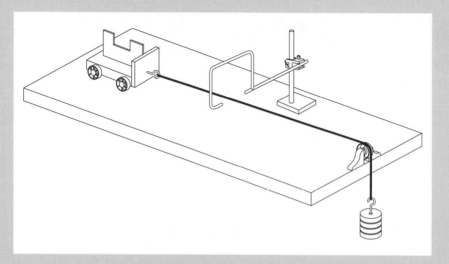

The student alters the force applied to the trolley by increasing the number of masses on the end of the string.

a **i** **State** the equation linking acceleration, change in velocity, and time. [1]

....

....

ii **Suggest** one measurement that the student must take in order to calculate the acceleration. [1]

....

....

COMMAND WORDS

state: express in clear terms

suggest: apply knowledge and understanding to situations where there are a range of valid responses in order to make proposals/put forward considerations

CONTINUED

b **i** **Identify** the independent and dependent variables.

Independent variable (the one you choose) [1]

....

The dependent variable (the one you measure) [1]

....

ii Suggest one control variable for this investigation. [1]

....

The student conducts the investigation and records the results in a table.

Force / N	Acceleration / m/s^2
2	3.8
4	8.1
6	11.6
8	15.9
10	19.8
12	23.6
14	28.4

c **i** Use the student's results to plot a graph of acceleration against force. [5]

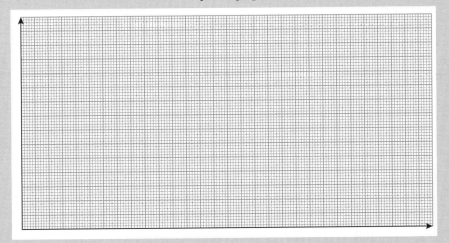

CONTINUED

> ii **Comment** on the relationship between acceleration and force on the trolley. Use your graph to **justify** your answer. [2]
>
> ....
>
> ....
>
> iii The gradient of the graph represents $\frac{1}{m}$ where m is the mass of the trolley. **Calculate** the mass of the trolley. [3]
>
> ....
>
> ....

[Total: 15]

COMMAND WORDS

comment: identify/ comment on similarities and/or differences

justify: support a case with evidence/ argument

calculate: work out from given facts, figures or information

Chapter 4
Turning effects

THE INVESTIGATIONS IN THIS CHAPTER WILL:

- allow you to describe the moment of a force as a measure of the turning effect of a force and calculate this moment for a variety of situations

- allow you to apply the principle of moments to determine if a system is in equilibrium or to determine an unknown variable. This is important in the engineering of suspension bridges

- allow you to determine the centre of gravity of regular and irregular shaped objects, and how the centre of gravity affects the stability of an object. The application of this can be seen in racing cars, which are designed to be close to the floor to increase stability.

Practical investigation 4.1:
The weighing machine

fulcrum: the point that an object rotates about or where it is balanced

mass: the amount of matter in an object

perpendicular: at right angle to something

weight: the force acting upon the mass of an object due to the pull of the Earth's gravitational field

moment = force × perpendicular distance from the pivot

IN THIS INVESTIGATION YOU WILL:

- use the principle of moments to build a weighing machine with force acting on both sides of the pivot, to determine the mass of a selection of small objects

- remember and use the equation to calculate the moment of a force.

- top-pan balance • metre ruler • prism or fulcrum • clamp stands
- two force meters • weighing pan • three small objects

Safety

- Secure clamp stands to a bench or the table to prevent them from falling over.
- Objects being added might fall, so wear full shoes to protect your feet from injury.

Getting started

The equation to calculate the moment of a force involves the force applied and the perpendicular distance from the pivot. In this investigation, you will need to ensure that the metre ruler is perpendicular to the bench.

There are different methods that can be used to determine if a piece of apparatus is at right angles to the surface. Research at least two of these methods and make some notes here.

....

....

....

Consider which of these methods you will use in your investigation to ensure the metre ruler is parallel to the work surface.

Method

1   Find the mass of the metre ruler and hence calculate its weight. Assume the centre of gravity of the ruler to be 50 cm from the pivot point.

2   Set up the apparatus as shown in Figure 4.1. Make sure your first object is in the balance pan, then move the two force meters to ensure the ruler is balanced. To get a correct reading, the force meters must be hanging vertically.

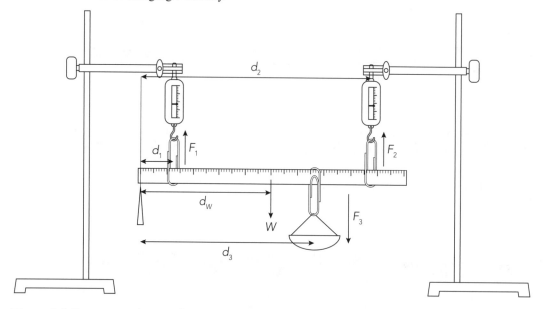

Figure 4.1: Experimental set-up for weighing machine.

3   Use an appropriate method to make sure the ruler is level, parallel to either the bench or the floor.

4   Record the reading on each of the force meters and their distances from the pivot. Record the distance of the object from the pivot.

5   Repeat steps **2–4** for a further two objects.

Recording data

1   Complete all the columns in the two tables. Work out the mass of the object by putting the total anticlockwise moment equal to the clockwise moment and solving the equation. Use $g = 9.8\,\text{m/s}^2$.

....

....

....

....

....

....

F_1/N	d_1/m	$F_1d_1/\text{N m}$	F_2/N	d_2/m	$F_2d_2/\text{N m}$	Total anticlockwise moment / N m

Anticlockwise

Total clockwise moment / N m	W/N	d_w/m	$Wd_w/\text{N m}$	F_3/N	d_3/m	$F_0d_0/\text{N m}$	Mass of object / kg

Clockwise

Analysis

2 Now take the objects for which you have calculated the masses and weigh them on an electronic balance. Record your results in the table.

Calculated mass / kg	Measured mass / kg

3 Is there a significant difference between your calculated and measured values of mass for your objects? Use data to support your answer.

....

....

....

....

Evaluation

4 The difference in your calculated and measured mass could result from the accuracy of your readings. Give two suggestions for how you could have improved your accuracy.

i ....

ii ....

5 During your investigation, you checked that the ruler was level (horizontal). Describe what you did to ensure this.

....

....

....

....

6 Why was it important to do this?

....

....

Practical investigation 4.2:
Finding the centre of gravity

IN THIS INVESTIGATION YOU WILL:

- design and carry out an experiment to determine the centre of gravity of an irregular 2D shape.

Getting started

When an object is disturbed, it will always come to rest balanced about its centre of gravity. It is easy to find the centre of gravity of a two-dimensional (2D) object with at least three lines of symmetry. It is at the point where the lines of symmetry cross. It is possible to use the idea that any object comes to rest balanced about its centre of gravity to determine the centre of gravity of a 2D object that has no symmetry. Research a method for how to find the centre of gravity of this type of object and note down your ideas.

....

....

....

....

....

....

YOU WILL NEED:

Write a list of all the items you will use during your investigation.

....

....

....

....

....

....

Method

Describe the experimental method to determine the centre of gravity of a 2D object with no symmetry. Your answer should include:

- how to set up the equipment

- how to conduct the practical

- how you will make sure you have accurate results.

- one safety consideration for this investigation.

You could include a diagram to help you in your explanation.

....

....

....

....

....

....

> ### TIP
>
> You can use a piece of card, or your hand, behind your 2D object to help support your drawing.

Analysis

1   The centre of gravity is at the point where the three lines intersect. You can check that your lines are accurate by placing your finger under the point where the lines meet. If the object comes to rest and balances, you have correctly identified the centre of gravity. Try this with your pieces of card. Are your lines accurate?

....

Evaluation

2   Explain how you could improve the accuracy of the lines you drew in your investigation.

....

....

....

REFLECTION

- Writing a method for another person to follow can be a challenge. Ask a friend to read through your method and try to follow your steps as they are written.

- Review your instructions. Choose two instructions that are not as clear as they could be.

- Re-write one of your instructions to make it easier to follow.

....

....

....

Practical investigation 4.3: Tower stability

KEY WORD

stability: the ability of an object to return to a stable position

IN THIS INVESTIGATION YOU WILL:

- design an investigation that will test the statement, 'The higher the centre of gravity of an object, the more easily it will topple on an incline'

- understand what is meant by centre of gravity

- determine what effect the centre of gravity of an object has on its stability.

YOU WILL NEED:

- metre ruler   • adhesive putty   • blocks (cuboids of uniform density)
- ramp   • protractor

Safety

- Wear full shoes to prevent injury to feet from falling blocks.
- Make sure that the end of your ramp is secure so that it doesn't slip off its support and trap your fingers.

Getting started

Set up the equipment listed. Consider the following points and write down your solutions.

Where will you measure the angle of the ramp from the bench?

....

How will you keep the height of the ramp stable?

....

How are you going to use the adhesive putty?

....

Where will you measure the height of the block from?

....

Method

Use the space provided to write your method. A table for your results has been provided in the Recording data section. Use this table to help you plan and write your experimental method.

....

....

....

....

....

....

....

....

....

....

Recording data

1   Record your results in the table.

Height of centre of gravity of tower / cm	Angle of topple / °			
	Attempt 1	Attempt 2	Attempt 3	Average

Handling data

2   Plot a graph of the angle of topple (on the vertical axis) against the height of the centre of gravity (on the horizontal axis). Remember to label your axes with the correct units and give your graph a title.

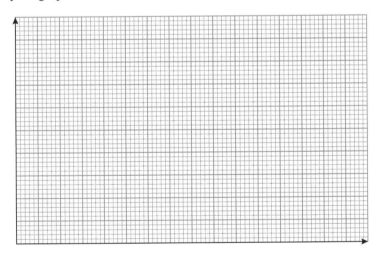

Analysis

3   Draw in a line of best fit for your results.

4   Does your graph support the statement in the learning intentions?
     Use information from your graph to justify your answer.

     ....

     ....

     ....

     ....

Evaluation

5   What other factors can affect the stability of an object?

     ....

     ....

     ....

     ....

     ....

6   How did you control these in your investigation?

     ....

     ....

     ....

     ....

     ....

7   In this investigation you used two measuring devices: a ruler and a protractor.
     State the precision of these instruments.

     Ruler ....

     Protractor ....

8   How could you improve the precision of the instruments used?

     ....

     ....

REFLECTION

- Reliability is the ability to reproduce results and ensure that they are not found by chance. Give one way in which you have made sure your results are reliable.

  ....

  ....

- With another group, discuss how you could improve your technique and how you might change the way you conducted the investigation should you do it again in the future.

EXAM-STYLE QUESTIONS

1 A student has been asked to investigate the principle of moments to calculate the mass of an object. He has been given the apparatus shown.

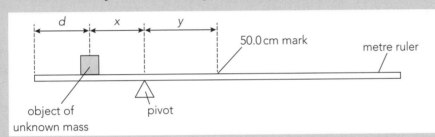

The student places the object of unknown mass a distance, d, of 15 cm from the zero end of the ruler, as shown. He adjusts the ruler so that it is balanced. The centre of the ruler is marked at 50.0 cm.

a i Measure the distance x from the centre of the object to the pivot.

   $x = $ .... cm   [1]

   ii Measure the distance y from the pivot to the centre of the ruler.

   $y = $ .... cm   [1]

b The diagram has been scaled 1 : 10. **Calculate** the actual values for both x and y.

   $x = $ .... cm   [1]

   $y = $ .... cm   [1]

> **COMMAND WORD**
>
> **calculate:** work out from given facts, figures or information

CONTINUED

c i The weight of the ruler is known to be 1.15 N. Use the principle of moments to calculate the weight of the object. Include the units in your answer. [3]

   ....

   ....

   ....

   ii Calculate the mass of the object and include the units. [2]

   ....

   ....

The student places the object on a balance and records the mass. Here is his result:

Mass of object = 149 g

d i **Give** two reasons why the answer the student calculated may not equal the measured mass. Assume that the experiment has been conducted carefully.

   1 ....

   ....

   [1]

   2 ....

   ....

   [1]

   ii **Explain** how you would ensure that the object was central over the 15.0 cm mark on the ruler.

   ....

   ....

   [2]

   [Total: 13]

COMMAND WORDS

give: produce an answer from a given source or recall/ memory

explain: set out purposes or reasons / make the relationships between things evident / provide why and/or how and support with relevant evidence

> Chapter 5
Forces and matter

THE INVESTIGATIONS IN THIS CHAPTER WILL:

- allow you to determine how forces affect materials, which impacts on the materials selected in industry, for example the material used for the cable holding a lift

- allow you to investigate the connection between force, pressure and area so that you understand why a sharp knife cuts through a tomato more easily.

> Practical investigation 5.1:
Determining the spring constant

KEY WORDS

anomalies: results that do not fit a pattern

elastic: the ability of a material to return to its original shape once a force is removed

extension: the difference between the original length and the new length of a material

oscillate: repeated up and down, or back and forth motion of an object

KEY EQUATION

spring constant, $k = \dfrac{F}{x}$

IN THIS INVESTIGATION YOU WILL:

> determine how the force (load) applied to a spring affects its extension by calculating the spring constant of a spring, using the equation $k = \dfrac{F}{x}$.

YOU WILL NEED:

- clamp stand and clamp • metre ruler • spring • 100 g masses
- G-clamp to secure the apparatus to the bench • safety goggles

Safety

- Secure the clamp stand to the bench to prevent it from toppling (falling over).
- Wear goggles to protect your eyes in case the spring snaps back.
- Wear full shoes to protect your feet from falling masses.

Getting started

Hang your spring from the clamp stand. Look at the spring carefully. Discuss with a partner where you might take your length measurements from. Discuss the following points:

- Why is it important to take the measurements from the same place every time?

- How could you adapt your equipment slightly to help you keep your measurements consistent?

Displace the spring slightly. How might the spring's behaviour alter your results? How will you ensure that you record accurate results given that the spring oscillates (bounces)?

Method

Use the space provided to write a method to investigate the effect of applying a load to a spring and its extension. Use the list in 'You will need' and Figure 5.1 as a guide on how to conduct the investigation. A table for results is provided.

....

....

....

....

....

....

Figure 5.1: Apparatus for determining the spring constant.

Recording data

1   Record your results in the table.

Mass / kg	Load / N	Original length / m	Stretched length / m	Extension / m
0	0			
0.1	1			
0.2				
0.3				
0.4				
0.5				
0.6				
0.7				
0.8				
0.9				
1.0				

Handling data

2   Plot a graph of load / N against extension / m. Remember to label the axes and choose a sensible scale.

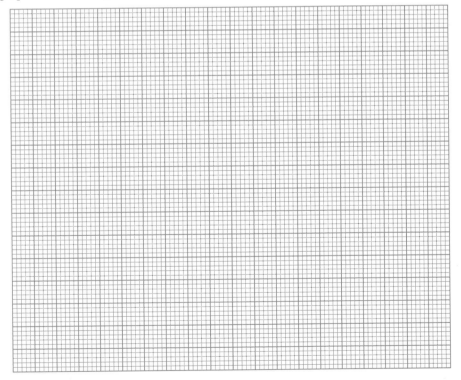

Analysis

3 Draw a line of best fit through the points on your graph.

4 Circle any anomalies in your results.

5 Describe the shape of your graph.

....

....

> **TIP**
>
> The extension of the material is directly proportional to the load applied if you have a straight-line graph through the origin.

6 Calculate the spring constant of the spring.

....

....

> **TIP**
>
> Remember that the equation for calculating spring constant is $k = \dfrac{F}{x}$.

Evaluation

7 Describe how the graph would change if you had continued adding masses to the spring.

....

....

8 Explain why this change in shape occurs.

....

....

9 Anomalies in results can occur due to inaccuracy in measurement. Suggest one reason why you might have obtained an anomalous result.

....

....

10 One reason for an error could be that the ruler used for measuring was not parallel to the spring. Describe a way in which you could ensure the ruler is parallel to the spring.

....

....

Practical investigation 5.2: Calculating pressure

KEY WORD

justification: reason why something is correct

KEY EQUATIONS

pressure, $\rho = \dfrac{F}{A}$

weight = mass × acceleration due to gravity

IN THIS INVESTIGATION YOU WILL:

- investigate how pressure changes depending on force applied and the area of a surface
- calculate pressure using the equation $\rho = \dfrac{F}{A}$.

YOU WILL NEED:

- centimetre-squared paper • pencil • high-heeled (stiletto) shoes • stool
- elephant's foot template • newton scales

Getting started

With a partner, write down the equation for pressure.

....

....

In this investigation, you will determine which of the following exerts the most pressure on the floor:

- someone standing on one foot

- someone walking in a pair of high-heeled shoes

- someone sitting on a stool

- a desk in contact with the ground

- a walking elephant.

Think about the surface area of each and the estimated force that each of these objects would exert and make a prediction about which you think will exert the most pressure. Order them from 1 to 5, with 1 being the greatest pressure:

....

....

....

....

....

....

Safety

Suggest one safety precaution you will need to take when conducting this investigation.

....

Method

1   Measure the mass of each object. For the mass of an elephant, research this using a book or the internet if you have access.

2   Place a piece of squared paper on the floor (or desk) and place the object you are testing on top of it.

3   Draw around the parts of the object that are in contact with squared paper.

4   Calculate the area by counting squares.

> **TIP**
>
> Include any squares that are at least half covered as whole squares but disregard any squares that are less than half covered.

Handling data

5   Using the equation for weight, calculate the weight of each of the objects and record this in the table.

6   Calculate the pressure applied by each object and record it in the table.

Object	Mass / kg	Weight / N	Number of legs	Area / m²	Pressure / Pa
school shoes					
high-heeled shoes					
stool					
table					
elephant's foot					

Analysis

7   Do your results support your prediction? Give a justification for your answer.

   ....

   ....

   ....

8   Give an explanation for why the pressure exerted by one elephant's foot is less than the pressure exerted by a stiletto heel on the floor. Use your results to support your answer.

   ....

   ....

   ....

Evaluation

9   Suggest one way you could improve the accuracy of your measurements of surface area.

   ....

   ....

REFLECTION

The method used for calculating the surface area of the objects is not as accurate as it could be. With a partner, discuss what issues you can see with the counting squares method.

Points to consider are:

- Did you both use the same method of estimation?

- Is there another way that the surface area could be calculated?

- How would the pressure calculated be affected if the area was smaller/larger?

EXAM-STYLE QUESTIONS

1 A student is investigating the relationship between the load (L) applied to a spring and its extension (x). The apparatus is shown.

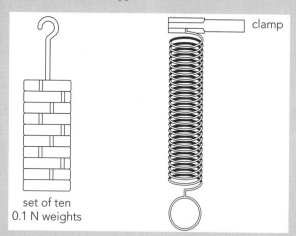

set of ten
0.1 N weights

clamp

a The student measures the original length l_o of the spring. Label clearly on the diagram where she should take the two measurements from. Label this length l_o. [1]

b The student takes some measurements and writes them in the table. Consider the measurements she should take and insert the correct column headings and units. [3]

0.0	0.0400	0.000
0.2	0.0415	0.0015
0.4	0.0430	0.0030
0.6	0.0445	0.0045
0.8	0.0460	0.0060
1.0	0.0480	0.0080
1.2	0.0505	0.0105

CONTINUED

c   Plot a graph of load against extension for the student's results.   **[5]**

d   The student suggests that load is directly proportional to extension.

   i   By reference to your graph, **state** whether or not the results support this statement. Give reasoning for your answer.   **[2]**

   Statement ....

   Reason ....

   ....

   ii   When recording the extension of the spring, it is important that the ruler is held parallel to the spring. State briefly how you would check the ruler is parallel.   **[1]**

   ....

   ....

   ....

   [Total: 12]

> **COMMAND WORD**
>
> **state:** express in clear terms

> # Chapter 6
Energy stores and transfers

THE INVESTIGATIONS IN THIS CHAPTER WILL:

- allow you to determine the gravitational potential energy of an object, a value that is required when considering the energy of falling objects such as bungee jumpers
- allow you to determine the kinetic energy of an object, a value which is needed to calculate the stopping distances of cars
- allow you to explain a simple example of energy conservation such as the simple pendulum in a clock or metronome used in music.

Practical investigation 6.1: Gravitational potential energy

KEY WORDS

gravitational potential energy (g.p.e.): the energy stored in an object due to its position on Earth. The higher the object the greater the g.p.e.

significant: a measurable difference that is not due to chance

KEY EQUATIONS

$\Delta E_p = mg\Delta h$

weight = mass $\times g$

IN THIS INVESTIGATION YOU WILL:

> remember and use the equation for the change in g.p.e., $\Delta E_p = mg\Delta h$, to determine the relationship between height and g.p.e.

YOU WILL NEED:

- ball   • top-pan balance   • string   • metre ruler

Safety

- Check the area is clear of trip hazards.

58 >

Getting started

When taking measurements of different quantities, it is important to consider the units you are using. In the equation for calculating the change in gravitational potential energy, the height should be in metres. However, rulers are usually in centimetres. To convert between centimetres and metres divide your answers by 100. For example, 10 cm = 0.1 m.

Practise converting the following measurements to metres:

5 cm   ....   65 cm   ....

32 cm   ....   87 cm   ....

Now try in the reverse, converting metres into centimetres:

0.26 m   ....   0.76 m   ....

0.34 m   ....   0.92 m   ....

Method

1   Use the balance to measure the mass of the ball. Record it in the space provided.

2   Drop the ball from the edge of the desk.

3   Use the string and the metre ruler to measure the distance through which the ball has fallen. Record it in the table.

4   Repeat for five different heights.

Recording data

1   Record the mass of the ball and the heights from which it is dropped.

Height / m	g.p.e. / J	Mass of ball = ...

Handling data

2 Calculate the g.p.e. for each of the heights, using the equation

$\Delta E_p = mg\Delta h$. Use $g = 9.8$ m/s^2.

....

....

....

....

....

Add these values to the table in Q1.

3 Use the data from your experiment to plot a graph of gravitational potential energy (vertical axis) against height (horizontal axis). Draw a line of best fit for your plot.

TIP
Choose a sensible scale, such as 1:2, 1:5 or 1:10 or a multiple of one of these.

Analysis

4   Describe the relationship between gravitational potential energy and height.
    Give reasons for your answer.

    ....

    ....

    ....

    ....

5   The gradient of the line on your graph is equal to the weight of the ball.
    Calculate the gradient of the line.

TIP
Remember that the gradient of the graph is $\dfrac{\text{change in the } y\text{-coordinate}}{\text{change in the } x\text{-coordinate}}$.

    ....

    ....

    ....

    Answer: ....   Units: ....

Evaluation

6   Calculate the weight of the ball from the measured mass and compare this to the weight
    calculated from the gradient. Are they significantly different? Give one reason why these results
    may differ.

TIP
Remember that weight = mass × g.

    ....

    ....

7   Suggest one other way to measure the height accurately.

    ....

    ....

REFLECTION

- Compare the results of your investigation with those of another group who used a different mass of ball.

- What conclusions can you draw about the effect of height of drop on the g.p.e. of the different balls you used?

....

....

....

Practical investigation 6.2:
Kinetic energy

KEY WORDS

kinetic energy (k.e.): the energy an object has because it is moving. The greater the kinetic energy of an object, the more difficult it is to bring it to rest. The stopping distances of cars are determined by their kinetic energy

reliability: the method will give the same result if repeated again

KEY EQUATIONS

$$E_k = \frac{1}{2}mv^2$$

$$\text{average speed} = \frac{\text{total distance travelled}}{\text{total time taken}}$$

IN THIS INVESTIGATION YOU WILL:

> remember and use the equation for kinetic energy, $E_k = \frac{1}{2}mv^2$, to calculate the kinetic energy of a tennis ball

- determine the relationship between the speed of a tennis ball and its kinetic energy.

YOU WILL NEED:

- chalk • tennis ball • stopwatch • metre ruler or tape measure
- force meter or top-pan balance

Safety

- Keep the ball in contact with the floor during rolling, to prevent collisions with other students.

- Take care when standing up after rolling the ball to avoid overhanging desk tops.

Getting started

It can be tricky when doing an investigation to know where to take measurements from. Usually scientists do a preliminary test to know what things can be hard to measure, or find issues in their method before they start.

Mark your start and finish line on the ground. Stand in a number of different positions near the end point and do a few trial rolls of the ball.

Discuss with your group:

- Which position will give you the most accurate result?

- How will you maintain this accuracy?

- What other issues might affect your result?

- How will you reduce the effect of these on your results?

Method

1   Use a piece of chalk to mark a starting line across the floor. Use the metre ruler or tape measure to measure a distance of 5 metres from this line and mark the finishing line.

2   Measure the mass of the tennis ball. Record it in the space provided.

3   Roll the ball along the floor. Use a stopwatch to measure the time it takes to travel the 5 metres from the start line to the finish line. Record it in the table.

4   Repeat step 3 three more times, increasing the speed each time you roll the ball.

Recording data

1   Record the mass of the ball.

Round	Time taken / s	Speed / m/s	$(Speed)^2$ / m^2/s^2	k.e. / J
1				
2				
3				
4				

Handling data

2   Calculate the average speed of the ball over the 5 metres. Record it in the table.

> **TIP**
>
> Remember the equation to calculate average speed $= \dfrac{\text{total distance travelled}}{\text{total time taken}}$.

3   Calculate (speed)^2 and the k.e. for each round and record it in the table.

4   Use the data from your experiment to plot a graph of kinetic energy (on the vertical axis) against (speed)^2 (on the horizontal axis). Label your axes clearly and include the appropriate units. Draw a line of best fit for your plot.

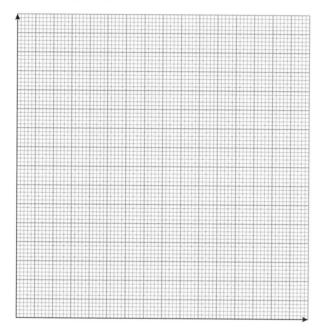

Analysis

5   Describe the relationship between kinetic energy and (speed)^2. Give reasons, with reference to your graph.

....

....

....

....

Evaluation

6 State one difficulty you encountered in taking accurate measurements. Suggest how you could have improved your experimental method to reduce this.

Difficulty encountered ....

Improvement ....

7 Comment on the quality of your results. Suggest one way in which you could have improved the reliability of your results.

....

....

....

....

....

8 How could you adapt this investigation to test the relationship between mass and kinetic energy?

....

....

....

....

....

....

Practical investigation 6.3:
Energy and the pendulum

KEY WORDS

anomalous results: results that do not fit a pattern

pendulum: a weight on the end of a fixed line. It swings, constantly transferring its energy between gravitational potential energy (g.p.e.) and kinetic energy (k.e.)

> **KEY EQUATIONS**

$E_k = \frac{1}{2}mv^2$

$\Delta E_p = mg\Delta h$

IN THIS INVESTIGATION YOU WILL:

> remember and use the equation $E_k = 1/2mv^2$ to calculate the kinetic energy of a pendulum

> remember and use the equation $\Delta E_p = mg\Delta h$ to calculate the g.p.e. of a pendulum

> use the conservation of energy to determine the link between g.p.e. and k.e. for a simple pendulum.

YOU WILL NEED:

• pendulum • clamp stand • clamp to secure clamp stand • top-pan balance
• light gate connected to a data logger (Figure 6.1) • 2.0 cm interrupt card • ruler

Safety

• Clamp the clamp stand to the desk to prevent toppling.

• Take care when swinging the pendulum to ensure it doesn't collide with the data logger or another student.

Getting started

In the space below, write the principle of conservation of energy:

....

....

....

Use this principle to predict the relationship between g.p.e. and k.e. in a simple pendulum:

As the height of the pendulum increases, the velocity will ....

Therefore, as the g.p.e. increases, the k.e. ....

Method

1   Measure the mass of the pendulum bob. Record its mass in the space provided.

2   Set up the apparatus as shown in Figure 6.1. Ensure the light gate is set up to record the velocity of the pendulum, using the interrupt card.

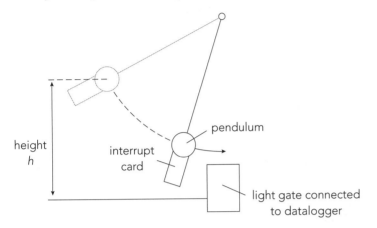

Figure 6.1: Experimental set-up for pendulum and light gate.

3   Raise the pendulum to the starting height of 5 cm. Measure from the beam on the light gate to the centre of the pendulum bob (see Figure 6.1).

4   Release the pendulum and allow it to swing freely, ensuring it passes through the light gate. Record its velocity as it passes through. Write it in the table provided.

5   Repeat step **4** twice more for this height.

6   Repeat steps **3** to **5** for five more different heights.

Recording data

1   Record your results in the table.

Height / m	Velocity / m/s				g.p.e. / J	k.e. / J
	1	2	3	Average		
0.05						

Handling data

2 Calculate and record the average velocity for each height of the pendulum.

3 Calculate and record the g.p.e. and the k.e. for each height of the pendulum.

4 Use your results to plot a graph of k.e. (vertical axis) against g.p.e. (horizontal axis) for each height and draw in a line of best fit.

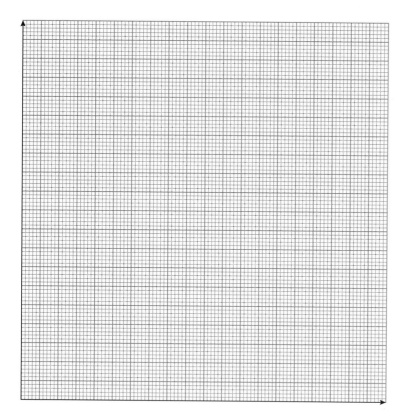

Analysis

5 From your graph, state the relationship between g.p.e. and k.e.. Give reasons for your answer, referring to your graph.

....

....

....

....

Evaluation

6 Were there any anomalous results? Explain how you would deal with an anomalous result.

....

....

....

....

7 Suggest two ways in which your method ensures reliable results.

1 ....

....

2 ....

....

REFLECTION

Some of the gravitational potential energy of the pendulum is transferred to the surroundings. State one way in which you could improve the experiment to reduce the amount of energy transferred to the surroundings.

....

....

....

1 A student is asked to investigate how a tennis ball rebounds on a concrete surface. The apparatus is set up as shown.

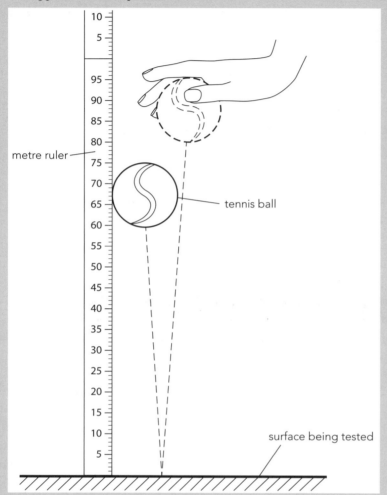

These are the student's results.

Release height / m	Rebound height / m			
	1	2	3	Average
1.4	1.07	1.02	1.04	
1.2	0.96	0.92	0.89	
1.0	0.78	0.74	0.73	
0.8	0.62	0.45		
0.6	0.42	0.49	0.47	

EXAM-STYLE QUESTIONS

a i   Read off the final reading from the diagram of the student's
        experiment and add the reading to the table.   [1]

   ii   **Explain** how you would obtain a valid average value for the rebound
        heights above.   [2]

        ....

        ....

   iii **Calculate** the averages and write them in the table.   [3]

        ....

        ....

                                                              [Total: 6]

COMMAND WORDS

explain: set out purposes or reasons / make the relationships between things evident / provide why and/or how and support with relevant evidence

calculate: work out from given facts, figures or information

> Chapter 7

Energy resources

THE INVESTIGATIONS IN THIS CHAPTER WILL:

- allow you to investigate how sunlight is used to generate electrical power and understand the advantages and disadvantages of its uses
- allow you to investigate the factors that affect the rate at which energy from the Sun is transferred, which can be used to determine the best type and position of solar heating panels on housing
- allow you to investigate and understand the concept of efficiency of energy transfer, which is useful in knowing how devices waste energy and how this waste can be reduced.

Practical investigation 7.1: Solar panels

KEY WORDS

control variables: the variables in the investigation that might affect your results if they are not kept constant throughout

dependent variable: the variable you will be measuring in your investigation

independent variable: the variable you will change in the investigation to see its effect

IN THIS INVESTIGATION YOU WILL:

- design an experiment to determine the relationship between the surface area of a solar panel and the time it takes to heat water.

YOU WILL NEED:

- metal food containers of different sizes • measuring cylinder • thermometer
- desk lamp(s) • metre ruler • stopwatch

Getting started

Before starting to plan an investigation, you need to identify all of the variables involved so that you can obtain a reliable set of results.

The variables have been identified for you:

- The independent variable will be the surface area of the solar heating panel.
- The dependent variable will be the temperature change in the water you are heating.
- The control variables in this instance are the time period, the volume of water, the material the solar panels are made from, the colour of the solar panels and the light intensity.

Discuss and determine with your partner the values you will use for the control variables:

Time period ....

Volume of water ....

Distance of light from the container ....

Colour of the solar panel ....

How often you will take temperature readings? ....

You will need to include these in your method.

Method

In this practical, you will measure the temperature change in the water in each metal food container over a fixed period of time.

You need to write a method for this investigation. This should be a step-by-step guide to what you will do in the experiment. It should include:

- what you are going to measure and the device you will use

- how you will set up the equipment to ensure accurate results

- your control variables

- the safety measures you will take.

- how you will record your results

The first step has been written for you. Fill in the blank and write the remaining steps..

1   Fill each of the metal food containers with .... cm³ of water. Rest a thermometer in each container. Align them side by side on the workbench.

....

....

....

....

....

....

....

....

....

....

Recording data

1 Record your results in the table.

> **TIP**
>
> Once you have put the units in a table heading, you DO NOT NEED to include them next to your values in the table.

Surface area of container / cm²	Starting temperature / °C	Final temperature / °C	Change in temperature / °C

Analysis

2 Write a conclusion for the relationship between the surface area of the solar panel and the change in temperature of the water for the water to heat. Use your data to justify your answer.

....

....

....

....

Evaluation

3 Why was it important to use the same volume of water in each solar panel?

....

....

4 Why might using one lamp for three solar panels in the investigation be an issue? Give reasons for your answer.

....

....

....

- Discuss how you conducted your investigation with another group. Write down one thing that you have learnt from how the other group conducted their investigation.

....

....

- Could the thing you learnt from the other group have improved your investigation? What impact might this have had on your results?

....

....

Practical investigation 7.2: Solar buggies

IN THIS INVESTIGATION YOU WILL:

- investigate how certain factors affect the amount of electrical power generated from solar cells

- design an experiment to test the following statement: 'Solar cars in hot countries where the intensity of light is higher do not need to be charged for as long as those in countries where the intensity of light is less.'

Getting started

In order to design an investigation, you will need to first identify the two variables under test and the corresponding control variables. Use the information in the key words box to help you determine the variables in your investigation.

Dependent variable (the one you measure)

....

Independent variable (the one you choose)

....

Control variables (the ones you will need to keep the same)

....

....

You will also need to predict what you think will happen, based on your prior understanding of energy transfer and general science. What effect do you think the distance of the light source from the solar cells will have on how far the buggy travels? Write down your prediction.

....

....

....

Method

Write a method for your investigation. Include:

- a list of what you will need

- what you are going to measure and the device you will use

- how you will set up the equipment to ensure accurate results

- control variables

- safety measures you will take.

....

....

....

....

....

....

....

....

....

....

....

....

Recording data

1   You need to record your results in a table. Be sure to include any repeat measurements you may take. Draw up your table of results in the space provided.

> **TIP**
>
> When you record data in a table, you should always write the independent variable in the left-hand column. Record the dependent variables in the remaining columns. You must include table headings with the corresponding units assigned.

Handling data

2   Use the axes provided to draw a graph of your results.

> **TIP**
>
> Remember to plot the independent variable on the horizontal axis and the dependent variable on the vertical axis.

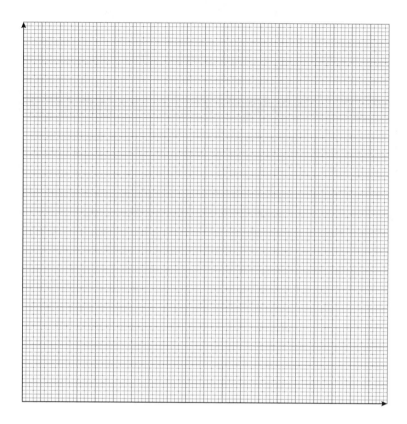

Analysis

3 Describe the relationship between the distance from the light source and the distance that the buggy travels. Use your results to justify your answer.

....

....

....

....

4 Do these results support your prediction? Justify your answer.

....

....

....

Evaluation

5   At the beginning of the investigation you were asked to list your control variables. How did you adapt your experiment to include these variables?

....

....

....

REFLECTION

Discuss and state one challenge you experienced during this investigation. Suggest one way you might change your method to improve it if you were to repeat this investigation.

Challenge   ....

Improvement   ....

....

Practical investigation 7.3: Efficiency of a tennis ball

IN THIS INVESTIGATION YOU WILL:

*   calculate the efficiency of a ball drop.

YOU WILL NEED:

*   tennis ball   *   measuring tape, or two 1 m rulers   *   clamp stand   *   retort stand
*   small step or something to stand on   *   set square   *   safety goggles

Safety

Wear goggles to protect your eyes from the rebounding ball.

Getting started

In this investigation it can be a challenge to measure both the drop height and the rebound height with accuracy.

Practise dropping the ball from a height of 1 m and recording the height of the rebound.

Consider the challenges you face in recording the height of the rebound. Write down how you are going to adapt your investigation in response to these challenges.

....

....

Method

1　Place the two 1 m rulers in the clamp stands, one above the other, with no gap in between.

2　Use a set square to ensure that they are positioned correctly, at right angles to the bench or floor.

3　Hold the ball at 1.5 m from the ground. Release the ball.

4　Record the rebound height of the ball in the table below.

5　Repeat steps **3** and **4** twice more for this height.

6　Now repeat steps **3** to **5** for different drop heights.

Recording data

1　Record your results in the table.

Drop height / m	Rebound height / m				Efficiency of the bounce
	Attempt 1	Attempt 2	Attempt 3	Average	
1.5					

Handling data

2　Using your results, calculate the average rebound height and complete the table.

3　Calculate the efficiency of the bounce for your ball by using the equation for efficiency:

$$\text{efficiency} = \frac{\text{rebound height}}{\text{drop height}}$$

4   Describe the trend that you notice in your results. Use the information in the table to justify
    your answer.

    ....

    ....

    ....

Evaluation

5   Consider the equation for the investigation. Why is only the drop height and the rebound height
    necessary to calculate the efficiency?

    ....

    ....

    ....

6   Describe why using a set square will help improve the accuracy of your measurements in
    your investigation.

    ....

    ....

7   Choose one error in your measurements and suggest a way in which you could reduce this error.

    ....

    ....

    ....

EXAM-STYLE QUESTIONS

1   A student is asked to investigate the effect of light intensity on the ability of
    solar panels to heat water. The equipment is set up as shown.

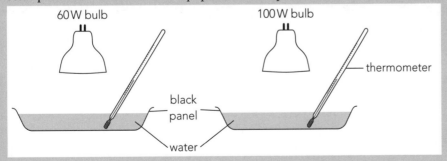

CONTINUED

The student starts the investigation. The thermometers display the readings for the 60 W bulb at 120 s, 240 s and 360 s.

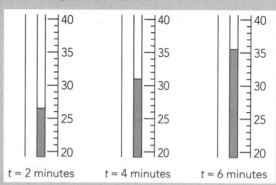

t = 2 minutes   t = 4 minutes   t = 6 minutes

a   Complete the table with the missing temperatures.   [3]

Time, t/s	Temperature, θ/°C
0	22.1
120	
240	
360	
480	40.0
600	43.5
720	49.0

b   **State** one way in which the student can obtain reliable results using good experimental practice. **Give** reasons for your answer.   [2]

Statement ....

Reasons ....

....

CONTINUED

c The student plots the results from the 100 W bulb on a graph.

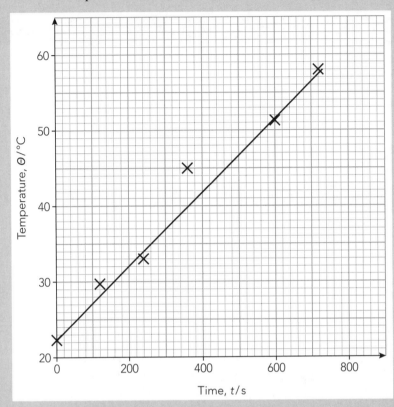

i Circle the anomalous result and give one reason why it might have occurred. **[2]**

....

ii On the same graph, plot the results for the 60 W bulb. **[4]**

iii **Describe** the relationship between light intensity and the temperature of the water. Use your graph to support your answer. **[2]**

....

....

....

[Total: 13]

COMMAND WORD

describe: state the points of a topic / give characteristics and main features

> Chapter 8

Work and power

THE INVESTIGATIONS IN THIS CHAPTER WILL:

- allow you to understand that mechanical or electrical work is equal to the energy transferred

- allow you to calculate the power as the rate at which work is done, so you are able to determine the energy emitted in a light bulb per second based on its power rating.

Practical investigation 8.1: Work done

KEY WORDS

precision: the smallest division of a measuring instrument

static: remaining still

work done: the amount of energy transferred from one store to another, for example, any time a force moves something in the direction in which it acts. Examples include lifting a book or an apple falling from a tree due to gravity

KEY EQUATIONS

weight = mass × gravitational field strength

work done, W = force × distance moved = Fd = ΔE

IN THIS INVESTIGATION YOU WILL:

- understand that mechanical working is equivalent to the work done

- remember and use the equation for mechanical working, $W = Fd = \Delta E$, to calculate the work done for different exercises.

Safety

Make sure you keep your back straight as you move into the squat to reduce the risk of back injury.

Getting started

Look at the exercises below. Consider how you will measure the distance travelled by the mass in each exercise.

Label the vertical distance travelled on each of the pictures.

- **Step-ups**: holding a mass at waist height, step up onto the step and then down again, as in Figure 8.1.

Figure 8.1: Step-up exercises.

- **Shoulder rise**: hold the mass in one hand and start with your arm down at your side. Raise the mass until your arm is straight above the shoulder. Return to the start position, as in Figure 8.2.

Figure 8.2: Shoulder rise exercise.

- **Static lunges**: hold a mass in each hand, with your arms at your sides. Assume the static lunge position in Figure 8.3. Move downwards into the lunge and return to the original position.

Figure 8.3: Static lunge exercise.

- **Squats**: hold a mass in each hand with your arms at your sides. From standing, move downwards into the squat and return to the original position, as in Figure 8.4.

Figure 8.4: Squat exercises.

- **Bicep curls:** start with your arm down at your side and raise the mass up until your hand is level with your shoulder. Return to start position, as in Figure 8.5.

Figure 8.5: Bicep curls.

Discuss how you will ensure the accuracy of your readings for each of the exercises.

> **YOU WILL NEED:**
>
> - a range of objects with different masses   • top-pan balance   • book   • metre ruler

Safety

Make sure you keep your back straight as you move into the squat to reduce the risk of back injury.

Method

1   Select the appropriate measuring instrument and measure the mass of the object being lifted. Record this in the table.

2   Use a metre ruler to measure the upward distance through which the mass will travel in one complete cycle of the activity. Record this in the table.

3   Perform the activity with 15 repetitions.

4   Repeat steps **1** to **3** for each activity.

Recording data

When recording data, it is important to include headings and the appropriate units of measurement. Fill in the correct units for the headings in the table below.

1   Use the table to record your measurements.

Exercise	Mass / ……….	Weight / ……….	Distance per repetition / ……….	Number of repetitions	Total distance moved / ……….	Work done / ……….
step-ups						
shoulder rise						
static lunges						
squats						
bicep curls						

> **TIP**
>
> When filling in your table, you should always use the precision of your instrument as your guide to the number of decimal places to which you record your observations. Use the same number of decimal places for each reading in the column.

Handling data

2   Calculate and record the weights lifted, using the equation

$$\text{weight} = \text{mass} \times \text{gravitational field strength.}$$

3   Calculate and record the upward distance travelled by the mass in each activity.

4   Calculate and record the work done for each activity using the equation for mechanical working

$$\text{work done} = \text{force} \times \text{distance moved.}$$

Analysis

5   Which of the activities transfer the most energy to the mass? Justify your answer.

……………………………………………………………………………………………………

……………………………………………………………………………………………………

Evaluation

6 When measuring the distances in your investigation, you will have taken your readings with your eye in line with the ruler at the point on the length you are measuring. Explain why you did this.

....

....

....

....

....

7 During the investigation, students who performed lunges or squats might have got tired. What effect could this have had on their results?

....

....

8 Why was it important to consider only the upward movement in all of the activities?

....

....

....

....

9 Wr down the names of two of the measuring instruments used and state their precision.

Instrument 1 ....   Precision ....

Instrument 2 ....   Precision ....

REFLECTION

With your group, discuss one improvement to the method that would ensure that the mass travelled the same distance in each repetition.

....

....

....

Practical investigation 8.2: Calculating mechanical power

KEY EQUATION

power, $P = \dfrac{\Delta E}{t}$

IN THIS INVESTIGATION YOU WILL:

- carry out an experiment to determine which student in the class is the most powerful, using the equation $P = \dfrac{\Delta E}{t}$.

YOU WILL NEED:

- bathroom measuring scales
- metre ruler
- stopwatch

Getting started

In physics, power is defined as the rate at which work is done.

In the space provided, write down the equation that links power, energy transfer and time.

....

Discuss ways in which you could measure the energy transferred and therefore calculate the mechanical power of your classmates.

Safety

Make sure you keep your back straight as you move into the squat to reduce the risk of back injury.

Method

Before conducting the investigation, you need to complete the table of results under 'Recording data'. Refer to the method to help you. A few of the column headings have already been included as a guide.

TIP

Remember that each column must have a heading and a unit of measurement.

1   Use bathroom measuring scales to measure the mass of each person. Record this in your table.

2   Calculate the weight of the person. Record this in the table.

3   Use a metre ruler to measure the change in the height of the student when they perform the squat. Record this in the table. Use Figure 8.4 from Practical investigation 8.1 to help you if you are unsure about where to take the measurements from.

4   The student starts from a standing position, moves downwards into the squat and returns to the original position. Time how long it takes for ten squats.

5   Calculate the total distance travelled during the ten *upward* movements of the squat.

6   Repeat steps **1–5** for other members of your class.

Recording data

1   Record your results in this table, when you have completed the headings.

Name	Mass /		Depth of 1 squat /		Work done /	Power / ....

Handling data

2   Calculate and record the work done for each student.

3   Calculate and record the power generated for each student.

Analysis

4   From your results, which student in the class is the most powerful? Give reasons for your answer.

....

....

....

5   Would it have been possible to predict the outcome of the investigation by looking at the
    weights of the students only? Justify your answer in terms of force, distance travelled and time.

    ....

    ....

    ....

EXAM-STYLE QUESTIONS

1   A student is conducting an investigation into which surfaces offer the least
    amount of friction, therefore requiring the least amount of work. She uses a
    margarine tub containing a weight and pulls it across different materials.

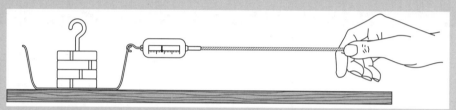

    She measures the force required to pull the tub at a constant speed over a
    distance of 50 cm.

    The readings for the four surfaces are shown.

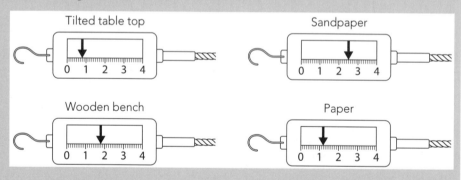

    a   Write down the readings shown, with the appropriate heading and unit,
        in the table.   [2]

Surface			
table top			
sandpaper			
wooden bench			
paper			

b Complete the table of results for the student's measurements and **calculate** the work done in the final column. [4]

The student realises that it is difficult to ensure that she pulls the tub at a constant speed.

c i **State** one precaution the student should take to ensure an accurate reading of force. [1]

....

....

....

ii **Explain** how you could adapt the investigation to reduce this issue. [2]

....

....

....

[Total: 9]

The kinetic model of matter

Practical investigation 9.1: Changes in state of matter

KEY WORDS

atom: the smallest unit of a material

molecules: a group of atoms bonded together to make the smallest unit of a chemical

particles: small portions of matter, for example, molecules, atoms, groups of molecules

relative: compared to something else

IN THIS INVESTIGATION YOU WILL:

- record observations of changes in state of a liquid.

YOU WILL NEED:

- tripod • heat source • heatproof mat • gauze • 400 cm³ beaker • 250 cm³ water • thermometer • clamp stand • clamp and boss

Safety

- Write two things that could be unsafe in this investigation:

  1 ....

  2 ....

- Write the precautions you will take for each of these things to ensure safety:

  1 ....

  2 ....

Getting started

In the boxes, draw the arrangement of particles in a liquid and a gas.

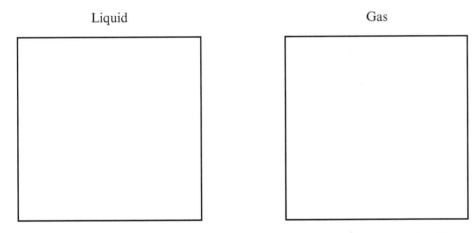

Liquid   Gas

With a partner, discuss and complete the table about liquids and gases. Use this table to help inform your observations and answers to the questions in relation to the investigation.

	Liquids	Gases
Bonds between particles		
Movement of particles		
Relative kinetic energy		

Method

Before starting this practical, read through steps **2–4** to ensure that you know what observations you are required to make.

1   Set up the tripod, heat source, heatproof mat and gauze. Put the water in the beaker and place on top of the gauze.

2 Place the thermometer into the beaker and clamp it securely. Record the starting temperature of the water in the results table.

3 Turn on and light the heat source. Heat the beaker on a roaring flame.

4 Measure the temperature of the water every minute for 10 minutes. Record each temperature in the results table.

Recording data

1 Record your results in the table.

Time / min	Temperature / °C
0	
1	
2	
3	
4	
5	
6	
7	
8	
9	
10	

TIP

Remember that all values in the table should be given to the same number of significant figures.

2 Watch the water as it begins to heat up. Record what you see.

....

....

....

3   How do you know when the water has started to boil?

....

....

....

4   Record the temperature when you think the water is boiling. Keep taking the temperature over the next few minutes. What do you notice about the temperature during this time?

....

....

....

Handling data

5   Sketch a graph of temperature against time on the axes provided. Identify any parts of the graph that represent a change in state.

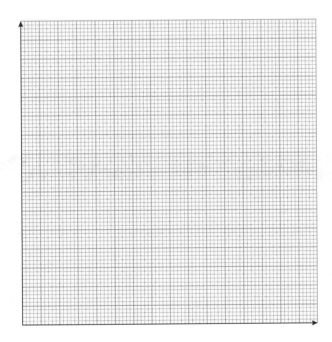

Analysis

6   Explain what happens to the kinetic energy of the molecules as the temperature of the
    water increases.

    ....

    ....

    ....

7   Explain, with reference to the energy being provided to the water, why your graph from
    question **5** has a horizontal section.

    ....

    ....

    ....

Evaluation

8   Why might it be difficult to take accurate measurements in this investigation?

    ....

    ....

    ....

REFLECTION

With a partner, discuss how you could improve the precision of your temperature
measurements in this investigation.

EXAM-STYLE QUESTIONS

1   A student is asked to investigate how temperature affects the amount of sugar dissolved in water. The student increases the temperature of the water and records the mass of the sugar that dissolves.

The apparatus for this investigation is set up as shown.

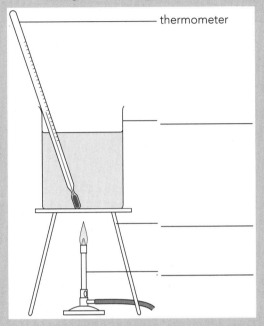

a   Fill in the missing equipment labels.   [3]

b   **State** two safety considerations that the student should follow in this investigation.

i   ....   [1]

ii   ....   [1]

The student records their results in the table below.

Temperature / °C	Mass of sugar dissolved / g
0	160
20	200
40	240
60	290
80	360
100	460

CONTINUED

c i Use the results in the table to plot a graph of mass of sugar dissolved against temperature. [5]

ii **Describe** the relationship between temperature and the mass of dissolved sugar. **Justify** your answer. [2]

....

....

....

d **Explain** why, with reference to the energy of the water molecules, the sugar dissolves more quickly in the hotter water. [2]

....

....

....

[Total: 14]

COMMAND WORDS

describe: state the points of a topic / give characteristics and main features

justify: support a case with evidence/ argument

explain: set out purposes or reasons / make the relationships between things evident / provide why and/or how and support with relevant evidence

> Chapter 10

Thermal properties of matter

THE INVESTIGATIONS IN THIS CHAPTER WILL:

- allow you to observe the thermal expansion of solids, like when a metal lid on a glass jar can be more easily opened by heating

- allow you to determine specific heat capacity of solids, enabling you to draw conclusions about which materials are best suited for a particular purpose

- allow you to investigate how surface area affects the rate of evaporation, which is useful when deciding the best way to dry clothes.

Practical investigation 10.1: Thermal expansion of solids

KEY WORD

capillary tube: a thin glass tube

IN THIS INVESTIGATION YOU WILL:

- observe how different types of glass behave when they are placed into hot water

- explain your findings in relation to the thermal expansion of solids.

YOU WILL NEED:

- tripod • gauze • heat source • beaker • water • ink • thermometer
- soda glass test tube • bung with capillary tube to fit test tubes
- laboratory glass test tube

Safety

- Stand up to conduct the investigation, to reduce the risk of scalds, if hot water is knocked over.

- Allow equipment to cool before handling, to reduce the risk of burns.

Getting started

Look at the equipment list and read through the method for this investigation.

Draw and label a diagram of the equipment set-up. Use scientific symbols to do this.

Method

1   Fill the beaker with water and place on the gauze on top of the tripod.

2   Place the thermometer in the water and observe what happens.

3   Heat the water to approximately 60 °C.

4   Fill the soda glass test tube with cold water that has been coloured with ink and place a bung with a capillary tube in the top, making sure there are no air bubbles present in the tube.

5   Place the test tube into the beaker of water and record your observations.

6   Repeat steps **3–5** for the laboratory glass test tube.

Recording data

1   Watch the thermometer after you place it in the beaker of water. Record what you see.

....

....

....

2   Watch the soda glass test tube after you place it in the beaker of water. Record what you see.

....

....

....

3   Watch the laboratory glass test tube after you place it in the beaker of water.
Record what you see.

....

....

....

....

Analysis

4   Explain why the liquid in the test tube with the capillary tube in the bung initially appeared to decrease in volume.

....

....

....

....

5   Why might this initial decrease be less in the laboratory glass test tube compared to the soda glass tube?

....

....

....

....

Evaluation

6   What can you conclude from your observations?

....

....

....

....

7   Have you ever struggled to open a glass jar with a metal lid? One way to solve this problem is to place the jar lid in hot water. The high temperature of the water causes the metal lid to expand but the glass jar does not. Explain why you think this is. Use the information from your investigation to support your explanation.

....

....

....

REFLECTION

Suggest any adjustments you might make to your method to improve the accuracy of your results.

....

....

....

Practical investigation 10.2: Measuring the specific heat capacity of aluminium

KEY EQUATIONS

$$\text{specific heat capacity} = \frac{\text{energy required}}{\text{mass} \times \text{change in temperature}}$$

$$c = \frac{\Delta E}{m\Delta\theta}$$

IN THIS INVESTIGATION YOU WILL:

> design and carry out an experiment to determine the specific heat capacity of aluminium

> use the equation $c = \dfrac{\Delta E}{m\Delta\theta}$ to calculate the specific heat capacity of aluminium.

YOU WILL NEED:

- 1 kg block of aluminium - insulating material - 50 W heater - thermometer

Getting started

Using the internet or a textbook, research a method for calculating the specific heat capacity of water. Write down the key points here.

....

....

....

Look at the experimental set-up in Figure 10.1. Research how you will use any of the equipment that you do not recognise. Write down what you find out here.

....

....

....

Method

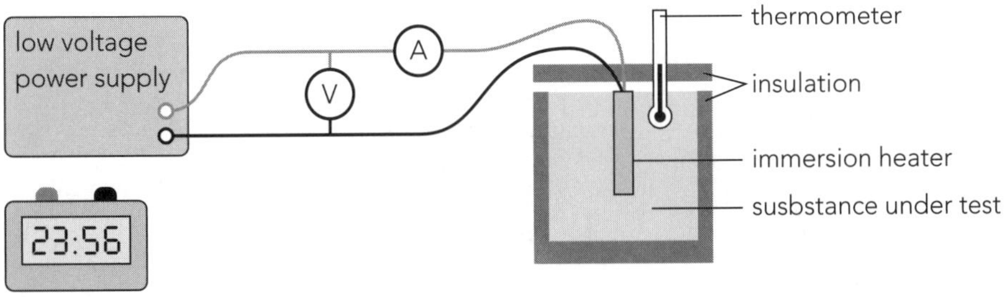

Figure 10.1: Apparatus for measuring the specific heat capacity of aluminium.

1 Using Figure 10.1 to help you, describe the experimental method for this investigation. Your answer should include:

- how to conduct the practical
- the measurements you will take
- how you will make sure you have accurate results
- two safety considerations for this investigation.

....

....

....

....

....

....

....

....

....

....

> **TIP**
>
> Think about the equations you will use to calculate the energy supplied and the specific heat capacity. Write them in the space provided and use these as a guide for the measurements you need to take.

2   Check your plan and carry out the investigation.

Recording data

1   Record your results in a table in the space below.

Handling data

2   Use the equation for specific heat capacity to calculate the specific heat capacity of aluminium, based on your results.

....

....

Analysis

3   Two different metals could be used to surround a set of PVC windows: aluminium or metal X. The specific heat capacity of metal X is 420 J/(kg °C). Compare this to your value for aluminium. Which material would you use? Give reasons for your answer.

....

....

....

4   Using either a book or the internet, look up the value of specific heat capacity of aluminium. Compare this to the value you have calculated in your investigation.

....

....

Evaluation

5   Suggest one reason why your value for the specific heat capacity of aluminium may differ to the one you have researched.

....

....

REFLECTION

Suggest one improvement you could make to the design of your investigation.

....

....

Practical investigation 10.3: Surface area and evaporation

Safety

- Stand up to conduct the investigation to reduce the risk of scalds, if hot water is knocked over.
- Allow equipment to cool before handling, to reduce the risk o f burns.

Getting started

In this investigation, you will be using containers with three different surface areas.

Look at the shape of your containers. Research the equations to calculate the surface areas of these shapes, and record your findings in the table.

Rectangle	
Circle	
Triangle	

Method

1   Measure the lengths of your containers and calculate their surface area using the relevant equation in the getting started section.

2   Measure 250 cm³ of water and empty it into the container with the smallest surface area.

3   Place the container on the gauze and heat until the water reaches 100 °C.

4   Allow the water to cool to 20 °C.

5   Pour the water into the measuring cylinder and measure the new volume.

6   Repeat for the other two containers.

Recording data

1   Complete the table with your results.

Container area / cm²	Volume of water after heating / cm³

Handling data

2   Calculate the volume of water that evaporated from each container.

Container 1 ....

Container 2 ....

Container 3 ....

Analysis

3   Look at your results. Make a conclusion about the relationship between surface area of container and volume of liquid evaporated.

....

....

....

Evaluation

4   Explain why it would be important for all of the containers to be made of the same material.

....

....

5   Suggest one way you could have improved the reliability of the results in this investigation.

....

....

REFLECTION

With a partner, discuss how you could have been more accurate in measuring the volume of water that evaporated. What would you do differently if you conducted the investigation again?

....

....

....

EXAM-STYLE QUESTIONS

1 A student is asked to determine the specific heat capacity of a 50 g sample of tiny balls of lead, known as lead shot. The student measures the starting temperature of the lead and records this in a table.

The student pours the lead shot into a 0.5 m tube that is sealed at one end. A bung is placed at the open end to seal the tube.

The student is instructed to hold the tube in the middle and invert it 20 times. The student then removes the lead shot and records its new temperature. The student then repeats this for a further number, *n*, of turns.

The student's results were recorded in the table.

No. of turns / *n*	Starting temperature	Final temperature	Temperature rise, θ / °C	Total energy transferred	Specific heat capacity of lead ....
20	22.8	23.6			
30	22.8	24.1			
40	22.8	24.6			
50	22.8	24.9			

a **i** Complete the table headings with the correct units. [2]

 ii **Calculate** the temperature rise for each value of *n*. [2]

COMMAND WORD

calculate: establish an answer using the information available

CONTINUED

iii The student realised that the energy transferred to the lead shot is
equal to the number of turns, n, multiplied by the gravitational
potential energy of the lead. Using the equation for gravitational
potential energy, calculate the energy transferred for each value
of n in the table.
Take $g = 10 \text{ m/s}^2$ [2]

....

....

....

....

b Use the equation for specific heat capacity to calculate the specific
heat capacity of lead for each of the attempts. (Hint: The gravitational
potential energy is equal to the energy transferred).   [4]

....

....

....

....

c The accepted value of the specific heat capacity of lead is 128 J/kg °C.
How do the student's results compare to this? **Give** reasons for
your answer.   [2]

COMMAND WORD

give: produce an
answer from a given
source or recall/
memory

....

....

d The student ensures that they wash their hands thoroughly after using
the lead. Why would this be a safety precaution for this investigation?   [1]

....

[Total: 13]

> Chapter 11

Thermal energy transfers

THE INVESTIGATIONS IN THIS CHAPTER WILL:

- allow you to conduct and design experiments to identify good thermal insulators which might be similar to those used in the development of reusable drinks cups

- allow you to determine how the colour of a material affects the absorption of thermal energy, a property that can be used in designing materials to reduce heat loss in homes

- allow you to describe the process of convection and apply the principle to novel situations such as weather systems

- allow you to identify the importance of colour in absorption of thermal energy, which is important for energy transfer in solar panels.

Practical investigation 11.1: Conductors of thermal energy

KEY WORDS

insulator: a material that does not transfer thermal energy easily

regulate: to help control

IN THIS INVESTIGATION YOU WILL:

- design an investigation to find out which materials are the best insulators of thermal energy.

YOU WILL NEED:

- four beakers • a sheet of each of the four materials to test • elastic band
- hot water • thermometer • stopwatch

Safety

- Take care when handling beakers, allow to cool before handling.
- Stand up when conducting the investigation to reduce risk of scalding.

Getting started

Materials for clothing are often selected based on their ability to help people regulate their temperature. In cold climates, materials are good insulators of thermal energy are chosen over good conductors, to ensure people are kept warm.

Which materials are known for being good thermal insulators? List them.

....

....

Which materials are used to keep things cool? List them.

....

....

Identify the independent, dependent and control variables for this investigation.

Independent variable (the one you choose)

....

Dependent variable (the one you measure)

....

Control variables (the ones you will need to keep the same)

....

....

Method

Describe the experimental method for this investigation. Your answer should include:

- a diagram of the experimental set-up
- how to conduct the practical
- the measurements you will take
- how you will make sure you have accurate results.

....

....

....

....

....

....

....

....

....

....

Recording data

1   Before conducting your investigation you need to consider how you are going to record your results. Placing results in a table is a clear and organised way of doing this. Draw up the table of results, ready for your investigation. Remember to include the appropriate units with any headings in the table title row.

Handling data

2   Plot a graph of your results. To make it easy to compare the materials, plot the results for all four materials on the same set of axes. You will need to remember this when selecting your scale. Plot your independent variable along the horizontal axis and your dependent variable on the vertical axis. Remember to label your axes, including the units.

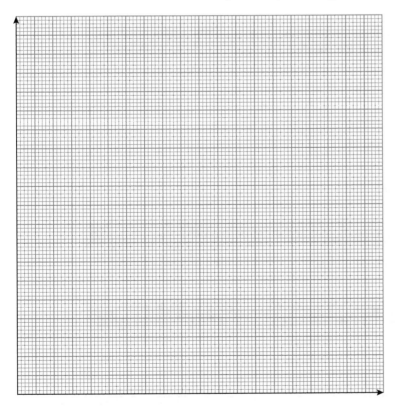

Analysis

3   From your graph, explain which material is the best insulator. Give justification for your answer.

....

....

....

4   Using particle theory, explain why you think this is the best insulator.

....

....

....

Evaluation

5   State one of your control variables and explain what measures you put in place so that it did not change in your investigation.

Control   ....

Measures   ....

REFLECTION

With a partner, discuss two ways in which you could have adapted the investigation to ensure your results were more reliable.

Practical investigation 11.2: Investigating absorption

IN THIS INVESTIGATION YOU WILL:

*   measure the rate at which thermal energy is absorbed by different coloured screens.

YOU WILL NEED:

*   radiant heat source   • black screen with stand   • white screen with stand
*   clamp stand   • silvered screen with stand   • petroleum jelly   • metal drawing pins
*   ruler   • timer

Safety

- Turn off the radiant heater when not in use to reduce the risk of burns.
- Allow screens to cool before moving and handle with care.

Getting started

Different colours absorb and emit thermal energy at different rates. In Practical investigation 11.1, you looked at absorption.

Based on your findings from Practical investigation 11.1, predict which of the coloured screens will absorb the most energy in this investigation.

....

How will you identify the screen that is the best absorber?

....

Method

1   Place a thin layer of petroleum jelly on the back side of each screen.

> **TIP**
>
> Petroleum jelly can be messy to handle and the pins may not stick as readily as you would like. Add more petroleum jelly if needed using a spatula.

2   Place five drawing pins on the back of each screen in the same orientation, and distance apart.

3   Place the black screen 5 cm away from the heat source. Position the screen with the black face towards the radiant heater and the pins on the back of the screen pointing away from the radiant heat source as shown in Figure 11.1.

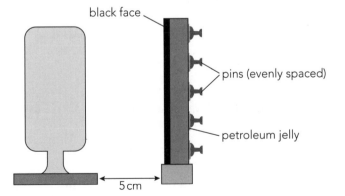

Figure 11.1: Apparatus to investigate thermal energy transfer by emission.

4   Turn the radiant heat source on and time for 5 minutes.

5 Record the number of pins that have fallen off the back of the screen at the end of the 5 minutes.

6 Repeat steps **3–5** for the white and silver screens.

Recording data

1 Complete the table with your results.

Colour of screen	No. of pins dropped
Black	
White	
Silver	

Analysis

2 Looking at your results, which of the screens is the best absorber of thermal energy? Use your knowledge of the impact of colour and radiation, and your results to justify your answer.

....

....

....

Evaluation

3 Consider the control variables in this investigation. Suggest two variables that may not have been controlled.

....

....

4 Suggest three ways in which would you alter the method to ensure that all variables were controlled as much as possible.

....

....

....

5   Explain why the screens need to be kept at a constant distance from the radiant heater.

   ....

   ....

   ....

6   Suggest an alternative method to measure the absorption of thermal radiation from each of the
   screen surfaces.

   ....

   ....

   ....

Practical investigation 11.3:
Thermal energy transfer by convection

IN THIS INVESTIGATION YOU WILL:

- observe and describe convection currents in the air when heated.

YOU WILL NEED:

- sheet of card   • pair of compasses (if available)   • ruler   • scissors   • string
- clamp stand   • clamp and boss   • heatproof mat   • two tea light candles

Safety
- Ensure the card spiral above the flame is positioned in such a way that it does not catch fire.
- Keep candles on the heatproof mat and handle with care to prevent risk of burns.

Getting started
What equipment do you have available that will allow you to draw a circle with an approximate
diameter of 10 cm? Try different options, before selecting the most appropriate equipment.

In this investigation, you will need to cut out a spiral from a circular piece of card. Consider how
you might do this as precisely as possible.

Method

1 On the sheet of card, draw a circle with a diameter of approximately 10 cm.

2 Cut into the circle, creating a spiral strip approximately 1.5 cm wide, leaving a central disk. Make a hole in the centre and thread a piece of string through the hole. Knot the string underneath.

3 Suspend the central disk of the spiral from the clamp stand.

4 Observe what happens without a tea light candle present.

5 Place a lighted tea light candle on the heatproof mat and observe what happens.

6 Add another tea light candle underneath the spiral and observe what happens.

Figure 11.2: Apparatus to investigate thermal energy transfer by convection.

Recording data

1 Record your observations.

Without a candle

....

....

With one candle

....

....

With two candles

....

....

Analysis

2   Use the kinetic model to describe why you think the spiral does what you have observed when the air is being heated by one candle.

....

....

3   Explain, using kinetic theory, why adding another candle might cause a change in the motion of the spiral.

....

....

....

Evaluation

4   Can you think of a variable you could test in this investigation?

....

....

5   How might a smaller diameter circle change your observations?

....

....

Practical investigation 11.4: Thermal energy transfer by radiation

KEY WORDS

aluminium leaf: very thin aluminium foil

vegetable black: a food colouring made of vegetable products

IN THIS INVESTIGATION YOU WILL:

*   observe whether black or silver coloured materials absorb more thermal energy.

YOU WILL NEED:

- radiant heat source • thermometer • white screen with hole and stand
- very thin aluminium leaf vegetable black • paint brush • clamp stand and boss
- tongs or wooden pegs

Safety

- Allow the radiant heat source to cool before handling it, to reduce the risk of burns.
- Use wooden pegs or tongs to handle thermometers to avoid the risk of burns.

Getting started

Think about what you know about the best absorbers of thermal energy. Make a prediction as to whether black or silvered material will absorb more thermal energy. Give reasons for your answer.

....

....

....

Method

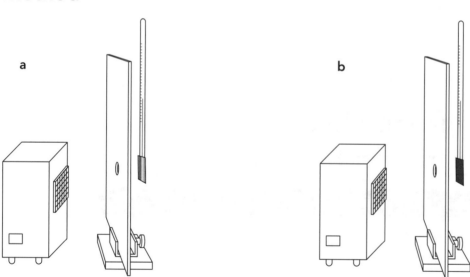

Figure 11.3: Apparatus to investigate thermal energy transfer by radiation.

1   Place the white screen in front of the radiant heat source.

2   Dampen the bulb of the thermometer with water. Carefully place the aluminium leaf onto the bulb of the thermometer as in Figure 11.3a.

3   Record the starting temperature from the thermometer.

4   Turn on the radiant heat source. Hold the thermometer with the aluminium leaf on the opposite side of the screen by the hole, so the heat can be felt.

5   Hold the thermometer in place for 30 seconds and then remove it. Record the temperature.

6   Allow the thermometer to cool.

7   Use a brush to apply the vegetable black to the aluminium foil as in Figure 11.3b.

8   Repeat steps 3–5.

Recording data

1   Record your results in the table.

Thermometer coating	Starting temperature / °C	Final temperature / °C	Temperature rise / °C
aluminium leaf			
blackened aluminium leaf			

Analysis

2   From your results, which of the two colours absorbs more thermal energy? Does this support your prediction? Give reasoning for your answer.

   ....

   ....

Evaluation

3   With a partner, discuss the validity of your results. Do you think it is possible to make a conclusion from this investigation?

1 A student was asked to investigate which of two surfaces was better at
absorbing thermal energy. The student was given two copper cans full of cold
water, a stopwatch, a thermometer and a heat source. One can had a shiny,
silvered surface, the other was painted matt black.

The experimental set-up is shown in the figure.

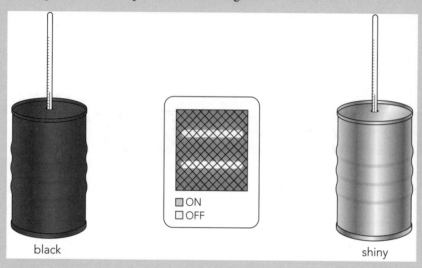

The heat source was switched on for 5 minutes. The temperature of each can
was recorded every 30 seconds. The graph on the following page shows how the
student presented the data.

CONTINUED

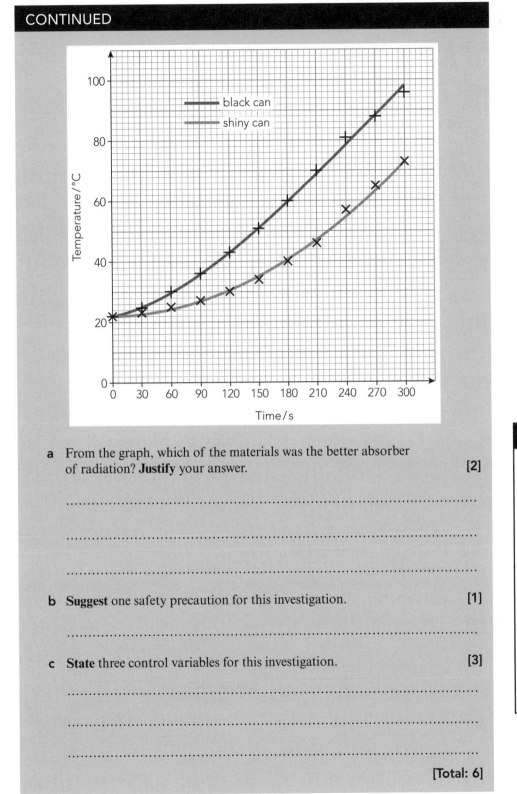

a From the graph, which of the materials was the better absorber of radiation? **Justify** your answer. [2]

....

....

....

b **Suggest** one safety precaution for this investigation. [1]

....

c **State** three control variables for this investigation. [3]

....

....

....

[Total: 6]

COMMAND WORDS

justify: support a case with evidence / argument

suggest: apply knowledge and understanding to situations where there are a range of valid responses in order to make proposals / put forward considerations

state: express in clear terms

CONTINUED

2 In a class investigation, students wanted to determine the impact of the material of a lid on reducing heat loss.

no lid   paper lid   plastic lid   reflective lid

a State the following variables for this investigation.

   i Independent variable (the one you choose) [1]

....

   ii Dependent variable (the one you measure) [1]

....

b State two control variables in the investigation. [2]

....

....

The students were asked to measure the temperature drop over a time period of 5 minutes.

c State the two pieces of equipment they would use to do this. [1]

....

d Suggest one way in which they could ensure that the temperature of each cup was measured at the same time. [1]

....

e Suggest one way in which they could increase the resolution of the readings of the thermometer. [1]

....

[Total: 7]

Sound

- allow you to investigate a method for calculating the speed of sound in air. An adapted form of this method is used in water to determine the depth of a seabed

- allow you to investigate how the medium through which sound travels affects the speed of the sound wave. This is important for the use of ultrasound imaging.

Practical investigation 12.1: Measuring the speed of sound

KEY WORDS

approximate: a value that is close to the true value

echo: a reflected sound wave

reflector: a surface that sound bounces off

rhythm: the regular repeated pattern of a sound

KEY EQUATION

$$\text{average speed m/s} = \frac{\text{total distance travelled/m}}{\text{total time taken/s}}$$

IN THIS INVESTIGATION YOU WILL:

- use a method similar to that of Sir Isaac Newton to determine the speed of sound in air

- determine the best types of surfaces for reflection of sound waves.

YOU WILL NEED:

- stopwatch   • metre ruler   • two blocks or hands   • reflective surface such as a wall

This investigation would, ideally, be completed outside, but an indoor sports hall or large corridor would also work.

Safety

If you are using blocks, make sure you hold them carefully, so as not to trap your fingers when you clap them together.

Getting started

It can be a challenge to find a good reflective surface. Before beginning your investigation, choose a few different surface types and practise reflecting your sound off them. Look at the type of surface and note down which surfaces work better than others in the space below.

....

....

What is similar about the surfaces that reflect the sound well?

....

Method

1   Stand as far away as possible (ideally about 50 to100 metres) from the reflective surface.

2   Clap your hands or the blocks together and listen for the echo. Adjust the rhythm of your claps so that you hear the echo before you clap again.

3   Record the time it takes for ten claps and echoes, (the first clap counting as zero). Start the timer as soon as the sound from the clap is heard and stop it when the echo arrives back. Calculate the time taken for one echo.

4   Decide on a reasonable number of repeat sets for the experiment and draw a table to record your data, in the 'Recording data' section.

5   Repeat steps 2 and 3 for your chosen number of repeat sets.

Recording data

1   Record the distance from the wall, in metres.

   Distance from wall = ... metres

2   Draw up a table of results for your investigation and record your data.

Handling data

3 From your data, calculate the average time taken for one echo.

....

4 Calculate the estimated speed of sound using the equation for speed.

....

Analysis

5 The recognised value of the speed of sound in air is approximately 340 m/s. Do you think your results are accurate? Give reasons to support your answer.

....

....

....

Evaluation

6 Explain why it is appropriate to use an approximate measurement of distance from the reflective surface.

....

....

7 Explain why, if we only consider random errors, the accuracy of your answers increases if you record the time taken for ten echoes to determine the time taken for one echo.

....

....

REFLECTION

- With a partner, discuss the challenges you think Newton would have faced in 1686 when trying a method similar to this investigation.

- Whose results do you think are most accurate: yours or Newton's?

....

Practical investigation 12.2: Sound through different substances

IN THIS INVESTIGATION YOU WILL:

- make observations on how the speed of sound changes in a solid and a gas

> use your knowledge of the arrangement of particles in a solid, liquid and gas to explain your observations.

YOU WILL NEED:

- wire coat hanger • two pieces of string or plastic film • metal rod

Safety

Wind the string comfortably around your index fingers to prevent bruising or damage to the finger.

Getting started

Predict whether sound will travel faster through a gas or through a solid. Give reasons for your prediction. Use your knowledge of the particle arrangement in solids and gases to help you.

....

....

Method

1 Set-up the equipment as shown in Figure 12.1.

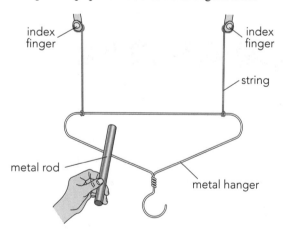

Figure 12.1: Wire coat hanger experimental set-up.

2 Wind a piece of string around each index finger. Hold the coat hanger out in front of you and ask your partner to tap the hanger with the metal rod.

3 Write down what you observe.

4 Now, with the strings still wound around them, place your fingers in your ears. Ask your partner to tap the coat hanger.

5 Record your observations.

> **TIP**
>
> Any metal object can be attached to the strings. Try with a spoon, or a tuning fork.

Recording data

1 Record your observations.

Fingers out of ears ....

....

....

Fingers in ears ....

....

....

Analysis

2 Explain why, when your fingers were not in your ears, the sound was difficult to hear. Use your observations to support your answer.

....

....

3 Justify the statement 'Sound travels faster through solids'. Make sure you include references to the arrangement of particles in a solid.

....

....

....

4   Predict how the speed of sound would differ if the coat hanger and the thread were placed in water rather than in air. Use your observations to support your answer.

....

....

Evaluation

5   State one issue that you had in this investigation that may have affected your results.

....

6   Explain how you could adapt your method next time to reduce any error this issue may have caused.

....

....

EXAM-STYLE QUESTIONS

1   A teacher is using a starter pistol to demonstrate to her class a method of measuring the speed of sound. She decides to fire the pistol, aiming at a reflector to produce an echo.

   a   **Suggest** something other than a wall that the teacher could use as a reflector in order to produce an echo.   [1]

   ....

   The teacher fires the pistol towards the wall 400 m away. She starts the timer as soon as the sound from the gun is heard and stops it when the echo arrives back. The display on the stopwatch is shown.

COMMAND WORD
suggest: apply knowledge and understanding to situations where there are a range of valid responses in order to make proposals / put forward considerations

CONTINUED

b i Write down the precision of the stopwatch. [1]

....

ii **Calculate** the speed of sound in air using the information provided.
Include the units of measurement. [4]

....

....

....

....

c Suggest one way in which the teacher can improve the reliability of the
results she has obtained. [2]

....

....

[Total: 8]

COMMAND WORD

calculate: work out from given facts, figures or information

> Chapter 13
Light

> Practical investigation 13.1:
Forming a virtual image in a plane mirror

KEY WORDS

normal: a line that is at a 90-degree angle to another line

parallax error: an error that can be caused when an object is not observed from eye level. It means that the value 'seen' looks different from the actual value. For example, reading the volume of a fluid in a measuring cylinder from above, or reading the speedometer in the car from the passenger's side (makes it look like the car is travelling faster than it is)

ray box: a light source that can provide a single beam of light or multiple beams

reflected ray: a beam of light after it hits a surface

IN THIS INVESTIGATION YOU WILL:

- make observations about the image formed in a plane mirror

- > describe how to form an image in a plane mirror.

YOU WILL NEED:

- power supply • ray box • multi-slit screen • plane mirror and mount
- A3 sheet of white paper • 30 cm ruler

Safety

- Ray boxes can become very warm after prolonged use. Allow the box to cool after use and handle with caution to prevent burns.

- Keep all electrical equipment away from water.

- Make sure your hands are dry before handling the electrical equipment.

Getting started

Turn on the ray box and place the multi-slit screen in the holder at the front of the ray box.

Place the ray box on a piece of paper. Practise drawing crosses inside the ray with a pencil. Try to ensure they are all in line with one another. Whilst it may seem easy, it can often be tricky to ensure they are all in a straight line.

Method

1   Set up the power supply, ray box and multi-slit screen on a sheet of paper, as shown in Figure 13.1. Place them opposite the mounted plane mirror.

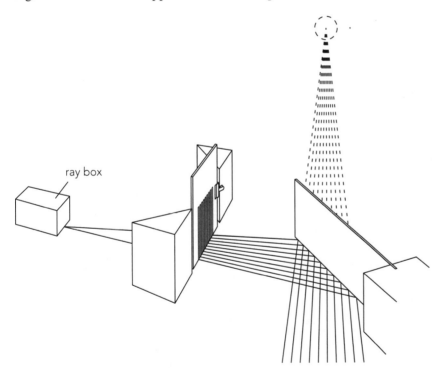

ray box

Figure 13.1: Ray box experimental set-up.

2   Turn on the ray box and align the slits so that the rays hit the mirror at an angle. Draw crosses on the paper along the incident and reflected rays..

3   Remove the ray box and, using a ruler and the crosses as a guide, draw the incident and reflected rays on the paper. Do this one ray at a time.

4 Now align a ruler with one of the diverging reflected rays. Trace its path behind the mirror, drawing it on the paper as a dashed line. Repeat this for all of the diverging reflected rays.

5 Where the lines cross behind the mirror is where the image appears to be coming from. Mark this as an image on your sheet.

> **TIP**
>
> When drawing the crosses, remember to do more than two for each line so that you can be as accurate as possible.

Analysis

1 State the law of reflection.

....

2 When representing light behind a mirror, why are dashed lines used, rather than solid lines?

....

3 Comment on the position of the image in comparison to the object, based on your investigation.

....

....

....

4 Summarise the four key properties of an image formed in a plane mirror.

   a ....

   b ....

   c ....

   d ....

Evaluation

5 In this investigation a multi-slit screen was used. Why would it be more difficult to find an image if you used a single-slit screen?

....

....

Practical investigation 13.2:
Finding the refractive index of glass

KEY WORDS

incident ray: a ray of light before it hits a surface (for example, the light ray that leaves a ray box)

normal: a line that is at a 90-degree angle to another line

refraction: the change of direction of a ray of light due to a change in speed as the light enters a different medium

refractive index: a number that tells us how quickly light passes through a material

KEY EQUATION

refractive index, $n = \dfrac{\sin i}{\sin r}$

IN THIS INVESTIGATION YOU WILL:

> use a common method of refraction to determine the refractive index of glass

> calculate $\sin i$ and $\sin r$ of an angle using a calculator

> determine the refractive index of a medium using the equation $n = \dfrac{\sin i}{\sin r}$.

YOU WILL NEED:

- semi-circular glass block • A3 sheet of white paper • power supply • single-slit screen
- ray box • protractor

Safety

Ray boxes can become very warm after prolonged use. Allow the box to cool after use and handle with caution to prevent burns.

Getting started

Using a protractor to measure angles can be a bit tricky if you have not done so before.

With a partner, practise using the protractor to measure the angles in Figure 13.2.

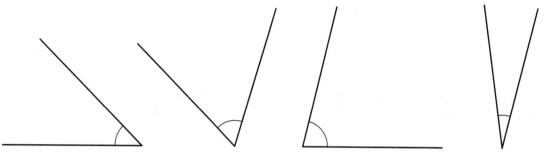

Figure 13.2: Angles practice.

> **TIP**
>
> Remember to line up the baseline of the protractor with the base line of the angle. Use either the inner or outer scale, whichever starts from 0 on the baseline, to measure your angles.

Method

1   Place the semi-circular glass block on the sheet of white paper and draw around the block in pencil to mark its position.

2   Remove the glass block and draw in a normal line through the radius of the semi-circular glass block.

3   Replace the glass block. Place the single-slit screen in front of the ray box and direct the single beam of light at the normal on the flat side of the block as in Figure 13.3.

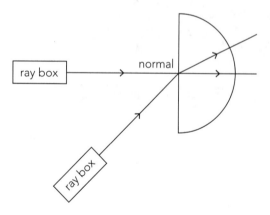

Figure 13.3: Ray box and glass block position.

4   Mark crosses on the incident ray and the refracted ray that comes out of the circular side of the block.

5   Using a protractor, measure the angle of incidence from the normal and record it in the table in the 'Recording data' section.

6   Trace the refracted ray back to the normal and measure the angle of refraction. Record it in the table.

7   Repeat for five more angles of incidence.

Recording data

1   Record your results in the table.

Angle of incidence / °	Angle of refraction / °	Sin i	Sin r

TIP

Ensure you know how your calculator works for calculating the sine of an angle. Also check your calculator is set to degrees.

Handling data

2   Calculate the sines of the angles of incidence and refraction. Record them in the table.

3   Plot a graph of sin *i* (vertical axis) against sin *r* (horizontal axis). Remember to label your graph correctly, including units where appropriate.

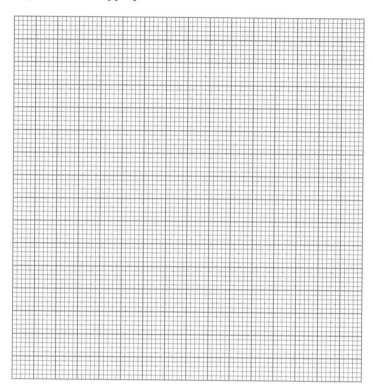

4   Draw in a line of best fit for your data.

Analysis

The refractive index of the material can be found by using the gradient of the line from the refractive index equation, $n = \dfrac{\sin i}{\sin r}$.

5   Use your graph to calculate the refractive index of glass.

    ....

    ....

    ....

Evaluation

6   The results of your graph should form a straight line. If not, the precision of your instrument could have affected your results. State the precision of the protractor you used in the experiment.

    ....

7   Select one of your angles of incidence. Calculate the sine of the angles that are one degree greater and one degree smaller than your angle of incidence, *i*. Plot these on your graph.

    ....

    ....

8   Looking at where these points lie on your graph, comment on the accuracy of the readings you have taken, stating one way in which you could improve your accuracy.

    ....

    ....

    ....

REFLECTION

- Discuss with a partner how you think this investigation went. Identify any areas where you think that you did not take accurate readings.

- What would you do differently next time to try to reduce the errors that you have introduced?

Practical investigation 13.3: Dispersion of white light

KEY WORDS

dispersion: separating light into the different colours it is made up of

normal: a line that is at a 90-degree angle to another line

IN THIS INVESTIGATION YOU WILL:

- observe the dispersion of white light when it is refracted by a glass prism
- determine the order of the colours of the visible spectrum.

YOU WILL NEED:

- power supply • ray box • single-slit slide • A3 sheet of white paper • 60° prism
- white screen and stand

Safety

- The ray box can become very warm after prolonged use, so allow it to cool before handling it.
- Handle the ray box with caution to prevent burns.

Getting started

In this investigation you will be using a 60° prism. Use a textbook or the internet to see what other types of prism you could use.

When white light is refracted it is split into a spectrum of colours. What order do you expect to see the colours in? List them below.

....

....

....

Method

1 Set up the power supply and ray box. Insert the single-slit slide in front of the ray box to form a single beam of light.

2 Place the prism on a sheet of white paper and direct the beam of light towards the centre of one side of the prism.

3 Slowly rotate the prism until the white light is separated and the spectrum is visible on the screen.

Recording data

1 Explain what happens to the beam of light as you rotate the prism.

....

....

2 Sketch how the spectrum appears on the screen, including the colours that you see, in the order that you observe them.

3 List the colours that were observed in the spectrum in the order in which they appeared.

....

....

....

....

Analysis

4 From your results, which of the colours of light was refracted the most?
Give a reason for your answer.

....

....

....

Evaluation

5 It can be quite difficult to see the spectrum when it first appears on the screen.
Suggest one way in which you could ensure the spectrum is clearly visible on the screen.

....

....

6 In this investigation you used a single-slit slide. Suggest a reason why a multi-slit screen has not been used.

....

....

7 Suppose another prism is placed in line with the spectrum of light. Explain what you might see on the other side of the second prism. Give reasons for your answer.

....

....

EXAM-STYLE QUESTIONS

1 Students in a physics class have been asked to investigate a converging lens. The apparatus is set up as shown.

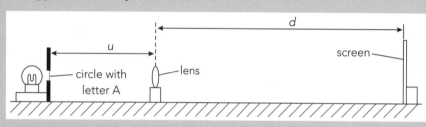

The screen is adjusted until a sharp image appears.

The object that is illuminated is shown.

CONTINUED

A student suggests it is possible to calculate the magnification by taking measurements of the distance between the screen and the lens, d, and the object and the lens, u.

a **i** Measure the distance d and record it [1]

....

ii Measure the distance u and record it [1]

....

iii Calculate the magnification using the equation: [1]

$$\text{magnification} = \frac{u}{d}$$

....

b **Suggest** two precautions the student should take to ensure accuracy in her readings. [2]

....

....

[Total: 5]

Properties of waves

Practical investigation 14.1: Waves on a spring

KEY WORDS

compression: an area in a longitudinal wave where particles are closer together

frequency: the number of times a wave happens in 1 second

longitudinal wave: a wave that vibrates (oscillates) parallel to the direction of energy transfer

rarefaction: an area in a longitudinal wave where particles are further apart

stationary: to be still

transverse wave: a wave that vibrates (oscillates) at right angles to the direction of energy transfer

wavelength: the distance between two consecutive peaks, troughs or same points on the wave

IN THIS INVESTIGATION YOU WILL:

- create both a transverse wave and a longitudinal wave using a spring

- identify the key features of waves and observe how they change.

YOU WILL NEED:

- large spring   • metre ruler   • stopwatch

Safety

Take care when releasing the large spring in case it causes injury on its return.

Getting started

Figure 14.1 shows the direction of oscillation of a transverse wave and a longitudinal wave.

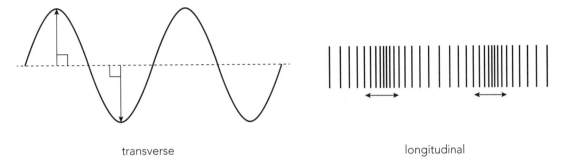

transverse   longitudinal

Figure 14.1: Direction of oscillation of a transverse wave and a longitudinal wave.

Use the large spring to practise how you will recreate these waves. Once you have created each wave, try to make the waves faster and slower.

Once you are confident with this, move on to the investigation.

Method

1   Work with a partner. Each take one end of the spring and stretch it out along the floor. See Figure 14.2.

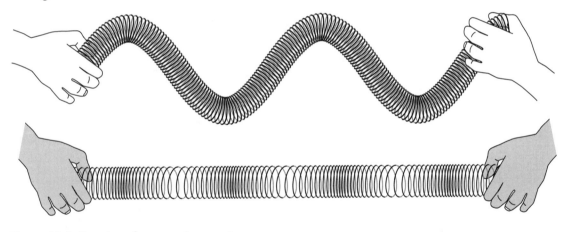

Figure 14.2: Creation of waves using a spring.

TIP
Pull the spring so it is loosely extended. Take care not to overstretch the spring.

2   Use the metre ruler to measure the length of the stretched spring. Record it in the table.

3   With the spring still stretched, one of you moves one end of the spring from side to side once, to form one pulse. The other should hold the other end of the spring so it is stationary. A transverse wave will be formed.

4 Record the time it takes for the wave to travel to one end and reflect back to the start.

5 Calculate the distance travelled by the wave.

6 Use the distance and time taken to calculate the speed of the reflected wave.

7 Repeat steps **1–6** for a longitudinal wave: quickly push the spring forwards and pull it backwards to generate a pulse.

> **TIP**
>
> Keep one end of the spring stationary at all times to ensure reflection at the boundary.

Recording data

1 Record the length of the stretched spring and the time taken for the wave to travel to one end and back.

Type of wave	Length of stretched spring / m	Distance travelled (twice the length of the spring) / m	Time taken / s	Speed / m/s
transverse				
longitudinal				

2 Sketch what a transverse wave looks like on the spring. Label the amplitude clearly on your diagram.

3 Increase the speed at which you produce the transverse wave. Note down what happens to the frequency and the wavelength of the wave compared to the first, slower wave you produced.

....

....

....

4   Sketch what a longitudinal wave looks like on the spring. Label a compression and a rarefaction.

Evaluation

5   In this practical, you were asked to record the time taken and the distance travelled by the wave. State one difficulty you encountered whilst making these measurements and suggest one way you can overcome it.

Difficulty ....

Solution ....

....

....

Practical investigation 14.2: Investigating the properties of waves

KEY WORD

ripple tank: creates water waves that are visible and which can be manipulated so we can observe wave properties more easily

IN THIS INVESTIGATION YOU WILL:

- observe and describe the reflection, refraction and diffraction of waves in a ripple tank

> observe and describe how diffraction through a gap is affected by both wavelength and the size of the gap.

> **YOU WILL NEED:**
>
> • ripple tank   • ripple tank barriers

Safety

If you have photosensitive epilepsy or have seizures triggered by flashing lights, you must speak to your teacher before the demonstration begins.

Getting started

Write down what you can remember about these three phenomena. Look out for these properties in the investigation.

Reflection	Refraction	Diffraction

Method

In this investigation, your teacher will use a ripple tank to demonstrate reflection, refraction and diffraction. Observe each demonstration carefully.

Recording data

Reflection

Your teacher will start by demonstrating the reflection of waves from a boundary.

1   Sketch a diagram of what you see. Remember to use straight, parallel lines to represent a wavefront.

2   Describe what you notice about the wavelength and speed of the wave once it has reflected from the boundary.

....

....

....

3   Describe how the angles of the incoming and outgoing waves are related.

....

....

....

Refraction

Your teacher will now demonstrate refraction in the ripple tank.

4   Explain why refraction occurred within the ripple tank when a raised shallow water boundary was placed in the tank.

....

....

....

5   What did you notice about the wave speed and wavelength of the wave after it had hit the boundary of shallow water?

....

....

6   Draw a diagram of the wavefront before and after it hits the boundary in the water.

Diffraction

Your teacher will now demonstrate the diffraction of waves through a gap.

7 Record your observations and draw diagrams to aid your explanation.

Wavefront passing through a large gap

....

....

Wavefront passing through a small gap

....

....

Analysis

8 Explain how the waves were formed in the ripple tank. Use a diagram to support your explanation if you wish.

....

....

....

....

9 Explain why the direction of a wave changes as it travels into shallower water.

....

....

....

10 In the diffraction demonstration, you observed waves passing through a small gap that was close to the wavelength of the wave. What conclusion can be drawn about the size of the gap in relation to the wavelength and the amount of diffraction that occurs?

....

....

....

....

Evaluation

11 Explain why it might be more difficult to observe the diffraction of light waves compared to the diffraction of water waves. Provide reasoning in relation to their wavelength.

....

....

REFLECTION

Look at the table you completed in the getting started section. Consider the following:

• Were you correct about the properties of reflection, refraction and diffraction?

• Were each of these properties visible during the demonstration?

• Can you think of a reason why they may not have been visible if you did not see them?

EXAM-STYLE QUESTIONS

1 A student is shown a ripple tank and asked to investigate the diffraction of water waves. The diagram shows the equipment the student was given.

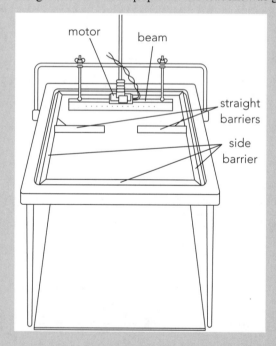

a **State** what type of wave is formed in a ripple tank. [1]

....

COMMAND WORD

state: express in clear terms

CONTINUED

b Write a brief method to describe how the student should investigate the relationship between the size of the gap and the amount of diffraction observed. The first step has been completed for you. **[4]**

Ensure the ripple tank is level and pour water onto the water table.

....

....

....

....

....

....

c i The student begins the investigation. She measures the wavelength of the wave to be 5 mm and the width of the gap to be 7 cm. **Sketch** what the student is likely to observe once the wavefront has passed through the barrier. The barrier has been drawn for you. **[2]**

7 cm

COMMAND WORD

sketch: make a simple freehand drawing showing the key features, taking care over proportions

CONTINUED

ii The student decreases the gap to 1 cm. Sketch what the student should observe once the wavefront has passed through the barrier. The barrier has been drawn for you. [2]

1 cm

iii **Describe** the relationship between the gap in the barrier, the wavelength of the wave and the amount of diffraction observed. [2]

....

....

....

d The student struggles to see the waveforms clearly when she adjusts the bar that creates the wave slightly. **Suggest** one thing she can do to ensure she sees the waveforms reliably. [1]

....

....

....

[Total: 12]

COMMAND WORDS

describe: state the points of a topic / give characteristics and main features

suggest: apply knowledge and understanding to situations where there are a range of valid responses in order to make proposals / put forward considerations

> Chapter 15
The electromagnetic spectrum

THE INVESTIGATIONS IN THIS CHAPTER WILL:

- allow you to determine which materials allow infrared radiation to pass through, which is useful information when selecting appropriate protection from infrared.

Practical investigation 15.1:
Investigating infrared waves

KEY WORDS

infrared radiation: an electromagnetic wave that is just beyond the red end of the visible spectrum

infrared transmitter: a device that emits thermal energy

IN THIS INVESTIGATION YOU WILL:

- devise and carry out an experiment to test which materials are good at absorbing infrared radiation and which materials are bad at absorbing infrared radiation.

YOU WILL NEED:

- infrared transmitter • infrared thermometer • materials to test • clamp stand
- clamp and boss • metre ruler

Safety
Never aim an infrared transmitter directly towards another student.

Getting started

Consider the different materials that you have in the laboratory. Which materials do you think will reflect, absorb or allow infrared radiation (an example of electromagnetic waves) to pass through?

....

....

....

Which of these materials are easy to source? Select four or five materials that you can easily test.

....

....

....

....

....

Method

Describe the experimental method for this investigation. You should include:

- the independent, dependent and control variables in your practical
- how to conduct the practical
- the measurements you will take
- how you will make sure you have accurate results
- how you will record your observations.

....

....

....

....

....

....

....

....

....

Recording data

1   Record your results in a table in the space below.

Analysis

2   Which of the materials blocked infrared waves most effectively? Give a justification for your answer, referencing your data.

   ....

   ....

3   In your investigation you selected a number of control variables. Explain one way in which your method allowed for these to be kept the same.

   ....

   ....

REFLECTION

- Read through your method. Change any instructions that you feel may be unclear to someone else trying to follow your method.

- Share your method with a partner. Ask them to show you any areas where they feel you have explained something really clearly.

EXAM-STYLE QUESTIONS

1 A student has been given three supermarket sunscreens. He has been asked to investigate which sunscreen provides the best protection from the Sun.

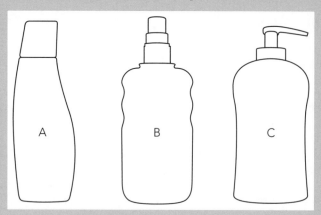

He decides to test the sunscreens by coating a clear sheet of plastic in the selected sunscreen and placing it between an ultraviolet light (UV) source and some fluorescent beads (small balls of plastic that fluoresce, or 'glow' when hit by UV light), to see if the UV light passes through.

a i **State** the dependent and independent variable for this investigation.

Independent variable (the one you choose) .... [1]

Dependent variable (the one you measure) .... [1]

ii **Suggest** two variables the student might need to control in this investigation to prevent these variables from affecting the result.

1 .... [1]

2 .... [1]

b The student was given several materials on which he could test the sunscreen. Suggest one reason why he might have chosen the clear plastic. [1]

....

....

....

COMMAND WORDS

state: express in clear terms

suggest: apply knowledge and understanding to situations where there are a range of valid responses in order to make proposals / put forward considerations

CONTINUED

c   The student conducts the investigation and records his observations in the table below.

Sunscreen	Observations
A	beads fluoresced slightly
B	no fluorescence
C	bright fluorescence

Another student suggests the results provided by the investigation might not be reliable.

Suggest one thing the student could do to improve the reliability of his results.   [1]

....

....

[Total: 6]

⟩ Chapter 16
Magnetism

THE INVESTIGATIONS IN THIS CHAPTER WILL:

- allow you to investigate the phenomena of magnetism, which has wide-ranging applications in the real world, such as the high-speed Maglev trains in China.

Practical investigation 16.1:
A magnetic circus

IN THIS INVESTIGATION YOU WILL:

- observe the forces in action when magnetic poles are placed together

- determine what materials are magnetic

- determine the field lines surrounding a bar magnet

⟩ understand that differing strengths of a magnetic field can be observed by different spacing between magnetic field lines.

YOU WILL NEED:

Station 1:
- two bar magnets with ends marked N and S

Station 2:
- bar magnet • copper strips • iron nails • steel ball bearings • nickel strips
- wooden pegs • aluminium strips

Station 3:
- bar magnets • plastic film • iron filings • an A3 sheet of white paper

Safety

- To avoid getting iron filings in your eyes, do not touch your face during the investigation.

- Wash your hands at the end of the session.

Getting started

Before conducting an investigation, it is a good idea to predict what you think might happen. This helps when you get a result you were *not* expecting as it gives you the opportunity to re-test to confirm the result.

Think about some everyday items that are useful because of magnetism. List them:

....

....

....

With a partner, discuss what sorts of materials they are made of.

Look at the materials list in 'You will need', for station 2. Predict which of the materials you think will be magnetic:

....

....

....

Think about these predictions when doing your investigation.

Method

Station 1

At this station you will investigate the forces between magnetic poles.

1   Place the magnets with their ends approximately 1 cm apart and note down any observations in the table. Repeat for the opposite ends.

2   Place one magnet on the bench, note which is the north pole and which is the south pole. Bring the other magnet towards it, pole to pole. Then reverse the second magnet and again, bring it towards the first magnet, pole to pole. Note any observations in the table. Reverse the first magnet and repeat.

Poles	Observations
N–N	
S–S	
N–S	

Station 2

At this station you will identify whether materials are magnetic.

1   Select a piece of material and bring towards the magnet.

2   Note down in the table if the material is magnetic or non-magnetic.

Material	Magnetic?

Station 3

At this station you will investigate the magnetic field lines around a bar magnet.

1   Place the piece of paper on top of the bar magnet.

2   Sprinkle the iron filings onto the white paper.

3   Sketch the pattern that appears around the bar magnet.

Analysis

1   What conclusion can you make from your investigation about the behaviour between the north and south poles of bar magnets when they are brought together?
    Give reasoning for your answer.

    ....

    ....

2 Describe the field pattern that you observed when placing iron filings in the magnetic field of a bar magnet. Include where you thought the magnet's field was strongest and how this was displayed by the iron filings.

....

....

....

....

3 Did the results of your investigation at station 2 support the prediction you made in 'Getting started'? Give reasoning for your answer.

....

....

....

4 At station 2 you tested magnetic materials. Write a conclusion for your results.

....

....

....

Evaluation

5 At station 3, you drew the field lines of a bar magnet, as shown by iron filings. It can sometimes be difficult to see the field lines, especially if the paper moves. How could you change the method to prevent this from happening?

....

....

....

6 How could you adapt the experiment at station 2 to see if any of the materials were magnets themselves? How would you be able to identify another magnet within the materials?

....

....

....

Practical investigation 16.2: Exploring magnetic fields

KEY WORDS

compass: a small round object with a magnetised pointer that points to North

demagnetised: when an object loses its magnetism

interaction: how two things behave in relation to one another

solenoid: a coil of wire in the shape of a cylinder that acts as a magnet when a current flows through it

IN THIS INVESTIGATION YOU WILL:

- use plotting compasses to observe the interaction of the magnetic field lines between magnets

- draw magnetic field lines of interacting magnets.

YOU WILL NEED:

- three bar magnets (one is for the extension) • white paper • plotting compass

TIP

Do not store plotting compasses near magnets. If plotting compasses are stored near magnets they may lose their magnetism.

Getting started

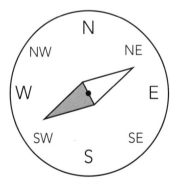

Look at the diagram of a plotting compass. Move around the room, holding a plotting compass. Notice what happens to the compass as you change position.

One end of the compass is either coloured or has an arrow. What does this end of the compass represent? Label it on the diagram of the plotting compass.

Method

1 Place two magnets, with a gap between them and with opposite poles facing, in the middle of a sheet of white paper on the bench.

2 Place a plotting compass at the end of one magnet. Mark two dots, labelled 1 and 2, on the paper to indicate the two ends of the compass needle of the plotting compass.

3 Move the compass a little further from the magnet, so one end of the compass needle is on dot 2 and mark the other end of the needle with another dot, labelled 3.

4 Repeat this process until you have mapped the field lines between the magnets and around each magnet.

5 Join the sequence of dots to show one field line around the magnet.

6 Repeat for magnets with the same poles facing.

Recording data

1 Sketch the results for opposite poles facing: N–S.

2 Sketch the results for same poles facing: N–N or S–S.

Analysis

3 Describe the pattern of the field lines you observed between the north and south poles.

....

....

4   Comment on where you think the fields are strongest. Use your results to provide reasons for your answer.

....

....

....

....

5   Predict what you think the field lines between three north poles arranged in the formation shown might look like. Draw your predicted field lines.

Evaluation

6   If plotting compasses are not stored correctly, they can become demagnetised. Suggest another material that could be used to illustrate the magnetic fields between two bar magnets.

....

....

....

REFLECTION

- With a partner, discuss the parts of this investigation that you thought went well. Identify the parts of the investigation that you found challenging. Why do you think this was?

- How could you have improved your investigative technique?

16 Magnetism

Practical investigation 16.3: Investigating electromagnets

IN THIS INVESTIGATION YOU WILL:

- consider the importance of electromagnets
- investigate two factors that affect the strength of an electromagnet.

YOU WILL NEED:

- two power packs • two lengths of insulated copper wire • steel paper clips
(The circuits will be set up for you and will just require switching on.)

Station 1:
- wooden core • steel core • soft iron core

Station 2:
- soft iron core • steel paperclips • extra-long piece of insulated copper wire

Safety

Turn off power packs when the electromagnet is not in use to prevent burns from overheating.

Getting started

Identifying variables is really important in investigations. If variables are not all identified, it could affect your results significantly. In the boxes provided, define the following variables.

Independent (the one you choose)	
Dependent (the one you measure)	
Control (the one(s) you will need to keep the same)	

Consider the investigations you are about to conduct. Write down a prediction for both stations.

....

....

....

....

Method

Station 1

At station 1, you will investigate the effect of the core on the strength of the electromagnet.

Write a brief method for this investigation. You should list the independent, dependent and control variables. You may include a circuit diagram if you wish.

The independent variable (the one you choose) is ....

The dependent variable (the one you measure) is ....

The control variables (the ones you will need to keep the same) are

....

....

....

....

Recording data

Station 1

1   You will need to record your results in a table. Draw a table of results in the space below for your investigation.

Analysis

Station 1

2 Write a conclusion for your investigation. Use your results to support your reasoning.

....

....

....

....

Method

Station 2

At station 2, you will investigate the effect of the number of turns of the coil on the strength of an electromagnet.

Write a brief method for this investigation in the space below. You should list the independent, dependent and control variables. You may include a circuit diagram if you wish.

The independent variable (the one you choose) is   ....

The dependent variable (the one you measure) is   ....

The control variables (the ones you will need to keep the same) are

....

....

....

....

....

Recording data

Station 2

3   You will need to record your results in a table. Draw a table of results for your investigation.

Analysis

Station 2

4   Write a conclusion for your investigation. Use your results to support your reasoning.

....

....

....

Evaluation

Stations 1 and 2

5   In station 1, you were asked to investigate how the core of an electromagnet affects its strength. Suggest one way in which you factored in your control variables in this investigation to ensure reliable results.

....

....

6   Why was it important to use only a soft iron core in the station 2 experiment?

....

....

7   How did you ensure that the number of paperclips picked up by the electromagnet was accurate?

....

....

REFLECTION

- Discuss with a partner why might it be important to repeat your results and then take an average when recording how many paperclips the electromagnet could pick up.

- Discuss the expectations of your results compared to what you recorded.

EXAM-STYLE QUESTIONS

1 A student has been asked to investigate the relationship between current and the strength of an electromagnet. The student has been provided with the articles shown and has to decide which of them to use to test this relationship.

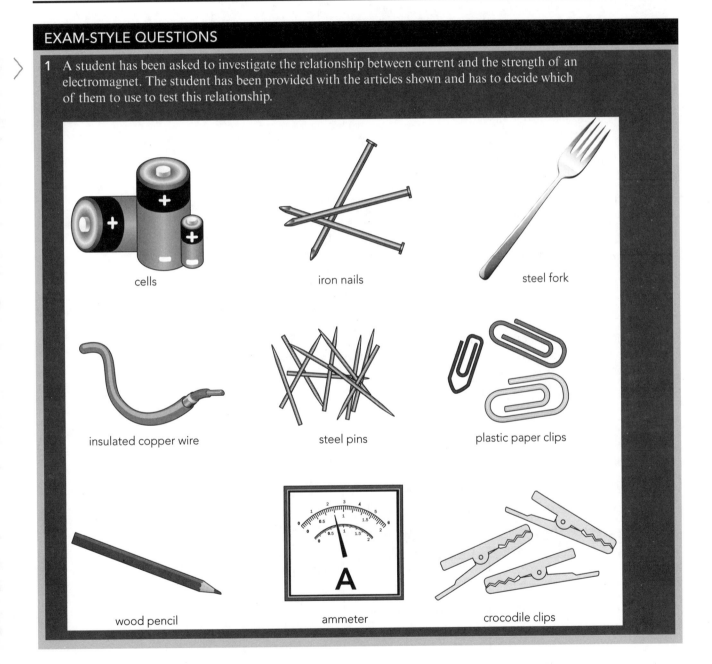

cells

iron nails

steel fork

insulated copper wire

steel pins

plastic paper clips

wood pencil

ammeter

crocodile clips

CONTINUED

a The student chooses to use a cell and the insulated copper wire to build an electromagnet. **Suggest** one way the student could strengthen the electromagnet without changing the current. [1]

....

....

The teacher suggested that the student places something inside the coil of the copper wire before starting the experiment.

b What item should the student choose as a core for the electromagnet? **Give** a reason for your answer. [2]

....

....

After selecting the core, the student chooses the plastic paperclips to measure the strength of the electromagnet.

c As he starts the investigation, he realises something is wrong. What does he realise? [1]

....

....

The student now uses the steel pins to measure the strength of the electromagnet. Before the student begins, he lists the key variables of the investigation:

Independent variable: current

Dependent variable: number of steel pins

Control variables: the core of the electromagnet

d Suggest one more control variable for this investigation. [1]

....

The results of the student's investigation are displayed in the table.

Current / A	Number of steel pins
0.2	4
0.4	8
0.6	9
0.8	24
1.0	36

COMMAND WORDS

suggest: apply knowledge and understanding to situations where there are a range of valid responses in order to make proposals / put forward onsiderations

give: produce an answer from a given source or recall/ memory

CONTINUED

e i Circle the result that you think might not be correct. [1]

ii The student conducted the investigation with care and attention.
Suggest one reason why he may have obtained this anomalous result. [1]

....

....

f Write a conclusion for this investigation. Use the data to support
your reasoning. [2]

....

....

....

[Total: 9]

> Chapter 17
Static electricity

THE INVESTIGATIONS IN THIS CHAPTER WILL:

- allow you to observe static electricity, created by friction, which you may have felt as a small shock when touching a car door

- allow you to design an experiment to find out which materials can be electrostatically charged, which will help you identify situations in real-life where things may become charged, such as an aircraft travelling through the air.

Practical investigation 17.1:
Investigating static electricity

KEY WORDS

electrostatic charge: a property of an object that causes it to attract or repel other objects with charge

insulator: a material that does not allow electrons to pass through

IN THIS INVESTIGATION YOU WILL:

- undertake an experiment to create and detect static electricity

- explain the properties of static electricity with reference to positive and negative charge.

YOU WILL NEED:

Station 1:
- two polythene rods • two acrylic rods • woollen cloths • watch glass

Station 2:
- salt • pencil shavings • woollen cloth • sheet of paper • balloon

Station 3:
- two balloons • string • piece of cloth • water bottle with sprayer

Safety

- When charging objects, take care not to stand on an insulating object, to reduce risk of static shock.

- Clean up water spillages on the floor immediately to prevent slippages.

- If you get any pencil shavings in your eye, wash out immediately with clean water.

Getting started

In this investigation, you will be charging up materials through friction. Not all materials will charge up easily and you will need to handle them with care to ensure they do not discharge.

Practise charging up the rods and the balloon with friction. You can do this by rubbing them with another material such as a cloth. If you have longer hair, you can check that the rods are charged by bringing them closer to your head and seeing if your hair stands on end.

Notice what happens if you over handle the materials once they are charged.

Method

Station 1

At this station, you will investigate the relationship between charged rods.

1   Rub the polythene rod with the woollen cloth and balance the polythene rod on the watch glass so that the rod can spin freely.

2   Rub the acrylic rod with another cloth and bring the acrylic rod towards the end of the polythene rod. Observe what happens. For example, does the polythene rod move? If so, in which direction? Record your observations.

3   Repeat this process for all combinations.

Recording data

Station 1

1   Record your observations in the table.

Rod combination	Observations
polythene and acrylic	
polythene and polythene	
acrylic and acrylic	

TIP
Once charged, handle the rods with only your fingertips and try not to touch anything else so that they remain charged.

Analysis

Station 1

2 Explain, with reference to charge, why you think the polythene and acrylic rods behave this way when brought together.

....

....

....

....

3 Explain, with reference to charge, why you think the other rods behave in this way when they are brought together.

....

....

....

....

Method

Station 2

At this station, you will try to use a charged balloon to separate a mixture of salt and pencil shavings.

1 Shake some salt and pencil shavings out onto the white sheet and mix together well.

2 Charge the balloon by rubbing it on your head.

3 Move the balloon over the salt and pencil shavings. Record your observations.

Recording data

Station 2

1 Describe what you observe as you pass the balloon over the salt and pencil shavings.

....

....

....

....

Analysis

Station 2

2   Why do you think this happens?

....

....

....

....

Method

Station 3

At this station, you will investigate what happens to two balloons when they are both charged.

1   Blow up the two balloons and attach a piece of string to each of them.

2   Hold the strings in one hand and allow the balloons to hang next to each other.

3   What do you observe? For example, do the balloons move? If so, in which direction? Record your observations..

4   Rub each balloon with the cloth and allow the balloons to hang freely. Record your observations.

5   Spray some water over each balloon. Record your observations.

Recording data

Station 3

1   Record your observations in the table.

Balloon condition	Observations
uncharged balloons	
charged balloons	
dampened balloons	

Analysis

Station 3

2 Once the balloons are rubbed with the cloth, they should move apart. Explain why you think this is happens.

....

....

....

3 Why might spraying the balloons with water reverse this effect?

....

....

....

4 Write a conclusion for the relationship between charges when they are brought together, based on the evidence provided by the observations in your investigations.

....

....

....

Evaluation

Stations 1, 2 and 3

5 Name one precaution you have taken in these investigations to ensure the reliability of your results.

....

....

6 Consider each of the stations you have just worked through. Were there any stations where the investigation took more than one attempt to work?

Reflect on your technique. How could you have improved your handling of the charged materials?

....

....

....

Practical investigation 17.2: Production and detection of electrostatic charges

IN THIS INVESTIGATION YOU WILL:

- devise and describe an experiment to determine which materials can be electrostatically charged by friction.

YOU WILL NEED:

- balloons • woollen cloth • concrete wall • wood • glass • small pieces of paper
- pencil shavings

Safety

Take care if touching your face during the practical, and wash your hands at the end to ensure that no pencil shavings reach your eyes.

Getting started

The materials available for you to test are: concrete wall, wood, glass, small pieces of paper, pencil shavings.

Using your knowledge of static electricity, write a prediction about which materials you think will experience an electrostatic charge. Give reasons for your prediction.

....

....

Identify the variables you will need to control in order to ensure your results are valid.

....

....

Method

Describe the experimental method for this investigation. Your answer should include:

- how you will charge the balloon
- how you will conduct your investigation
- any control variables
- how you will record your results.

....

....

....

....

....

....

TIP
When writing your method, ensure you include the instrument that you will need to use to take a measurement. For example, measure the distance using a 1 m ruler.

Results

Record your results in the space provided below using an appropriate table.

Analysis

1   Write a conclusion about the materials used in your investigation. Give reasoning based on your results.

....

....

Evaluation

2   As your body is a conductor, if you touch the balloon once it is charged you might discharge it. Explain how you adapted your method to ensure the balloon remained charged.

....

....

REFLECTION

- Partner up with someone else in the class. Read their method. Now read yours. Highlight anything that your partner has included that you could include in your method.

- Give each other suggestions on how you could improve your methods.

EXAM-STYLE QUESTIONS

1   Student A is in the laboratory experimenting with some electrostatics equipment. The equipment the student is using is shown in the figure.

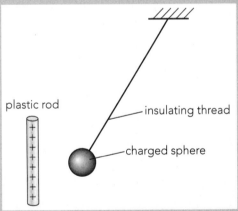

plastic rod

insulating thread

charged sphere

a   i   **Suggest** one way that student A could have charged the plastic rod.   **[1]**

....

Once the rod is charged, the charged sphere moves towards the rod.

....

COMMAND WORD

suggest: apply knowledge and understanding to situations where there are a range of valid responses in order to make proposals / put forward considerations

CONTINUED

    ii Suggest the nature of the charge on the sphere. **Justify** your answer.   **[2]**

....

....

b Suggest one material that the insulating thread could be made from.
Give a reason for your answer.   **[2]**

....

....

Student B discusses the apparatus with student A and suggests he should try the investigation on a wet day to get a better result.

c Do you agree with student B? Give a reason for your answer.   **[2]**

....

....

d The rod is now given a negative charge. Suggest what will happen to the position of the charged sphere.   **[1]**

....

[Total: 8]

COMMAND WORDS

justify: support a case with evidence/ argument

give: produce an answer from a given source or recall/ memory

Electrical quantities

- allow you to investigate and understand current in a series and parallel circuit; for example, current can be changed in a hairdryer to change the speed of the turbine
- allow you to explore the factors that affect resistance and use these to select for the correct component in a particular circuit to ensure it works effectively
- allow you to see how energy is transferred in circuits; for example, in motor vehicles, energy is transferred as light through the headlamps, transferred through mechanical work through the motor, and transferred as sound through the car stereo.

Practical investigation 18.1:
Investigating current

IN THIS INVESTIGATION YOU WILL:

- construct series circuits and parallel circuits
- observe and explain how current flows around series and parallel circuits.

YOU WILL NEED:

- two 1.5 V cells • two lamps • ammeter • connecting leads • push switch

Safety
Keep circuits away from water and ensure they are turned off when not in use.

Getting started
When conducting an electricity investigation, one of the biggest challenges can be identifying the reason why a circuit is not working. With a partner, discuss all the possible reasons for an incomplete circuit.

List them here:

....

....

Now test each component across the cells to ensure that they are working before building your circuit. Ensure all the lamps are screwed in correctly before starting.

Method

Series circuit

1 Set up the circuit as illustrated in Figure 18.1.

2 Record the ammeter reading in position 1.

3 Repeat for positions 2 and 3.

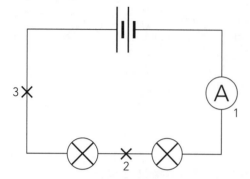

Figure 18.1: Ammeter in a series circuit.

Parallel circuit

1 Set up the circuit as illustrated in Figure 18.2.

2 Record the ammeter reading in position 1.

3 Repeat for positions 2–4.

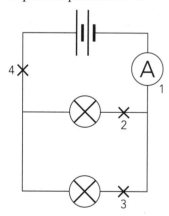

Figure 18.2: Ammeter in a parallel circuit.

> **TIP**
>
> When constructing the parallel circuit, construct one loop at a time, starting with the top loop or basic series circuit first. Then, add the second branch either side of the relevant component.

Recording data

1 Record your results for the series circuit in Table 18.1.

Ammeter position	Ammeter reading / A
1	
2	
3	

Table 18.1: Series circuit results.

2 Record your results for the parallel circuit in Table 18.2.

Ammeter position	Ammeter reading / A
1	
2	
3	
4	

Table 18.2: Parallel circuit results.

Analysis

3 Write a conclusion explaining how the current flows around a series circuit. Use your results to support your answer.

....

....

4 Write a conclusion explaining how the current flows around a parallel circuit. Use your results to support your answer.

....

....

5 A student conducts a similar investigation to this and predicts that the current will be used up as it travels around the circuit. Do you agree with this statement? Give a reason for your answer.

....

....

....

Evaluation

6   Name the device used to measure the current in the investigation in question **5**. Suggest a reason why a digital version might be better than an analogue version.

....

....

7   Imagine a push switch is inserted into this circuit. How might this make the circuit safer?

....

....

REFLECTION

- Describe to a partner how you made sure your second circuit was a parallel circuit.
- Explain what you found most challenging in setting this circuit up.

Practical investigation 18.2: Determining the resistance

KEY WORD

resistance: opposition to flow of charge

KEY EQUATION

resistance, $R = \dfrac{V}{I}$

IN THIS INVESTIGATION YOU WILL:

- devise an experiment to test the resistance of a number of resistors
- draw circuit diagrams to represent your experimental set up and construct and use these circuits
- calculate resistance using the equation $R = \dfrac{V}{I}$.

YOU WILL NEED:

- variety of resistors   • component holders   • leads   • two 1.5 V cells   • ammeter
- voltmeter   • push switch   • heatproof mat

Safety

- Replace any loose or damaged wires to prevent electric shock.

- Turn the circuit off when it is not in use to prevent effects of overheating.

Getting started

In this investigation you are going to determine the resistance of a number of resistors. In the space below, write down the measurements you will take and the devices you will need:

Measurement: ....   Device: ....

Measurement: ....   Device: ....

The position of each of these devices in the circuit will be important. Note down next to each component where you will place them in the circuit.

Method

Devise an investigation to calculate the resistance of the components with which you have been provided. Your method should include:

- a circuit diagram of the circuit to be set up

- how you will conduct the investigation

- what readings you will take and what instruments you will use to take them.

Space has been provided for you on the next page.

....

....

....

....

....

Recording data

1 Construct a table of results for your investigation in the space below.

TIP
Remember: your table should have headings and units where relevant.

Analysis

2 Based on your results, calculate the resistance of the resistors you have tested.

....

....

3   Check the colour code of the resistor against a resistor identification table, which you can find on the internet or in the resistor pack. Are your results similar to the accepted value of the resistor? Give a reason for your answer.

....

....

Evaluation

4   State the precision of the voltmeter and ammeter used in your investigation.

Ammeter ....

Voltmeter ....

REFLECTION

- With a partner, discuss how reliable the results in this experiment are.
- How could you adapt this investigation to ensure you have more reliable results?

Practical investigation 18.3: Investigating current in components

---

KEY WORDS

thermistor: a temperature-dependent resistor

zero error: when a measuring device does not start at 0

IN THIS INVESTIGATION YOU WILL:

- take accurate measurements of current and potential difference in a circuit with varying resistance
- draw a graph of current against p.d. and comment on the relationship between these two variables.

YOU WILL NEED:

- 100 Ω resistor • component holder • leads • heatproof mat • ammeter
- voltmeter • power supply • variable resistor

Safety

- Turn power packs off when they are not in use to prevent overheating in the resistor.
- Place a heatproof mat underneath the resistor to prevent damage to the workbench surface.

Getting started

Before conducting an investigation, is it useful to do a practice run. Set up your circuit and experiment with changing the position of the sliding contact on the variable resistor to see if the current values will give you a large enough range from which to plot a graph.

Perhaps try going up in 0.25 V, 0.5 V, then 1 V to see which gives you a nice spread of results for current.

Use these early readings to fix your range of potential difference values.

Method

1   Set up the circuit as shown in Figure 18.3, placing the heatproof mat underneath the resistor.

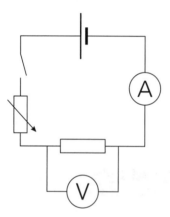

Figure 18.3: Circuit diagram for investigating current.

2   Select a range of p.d.s including 0 V and up to 5 V.

3   Turn on the circuit with the variable resistor in position for the highest p.d. Record the p.d. and current readings in your table.

4   Turn off the circuit when it is not in use.

5   Repeat for five more readings of p.d. and current.

6   Reverse the polarity of the current by switching the connecting cables attached to the cell or power supply in the component holder. Repeat steps **1–5** for negative values of p.d.

Recording data

1   Draw a table of results for your investigation in the space below.

Handling data

2   Use your results to draw a graph of current, *I*, against potential difference, *V*.

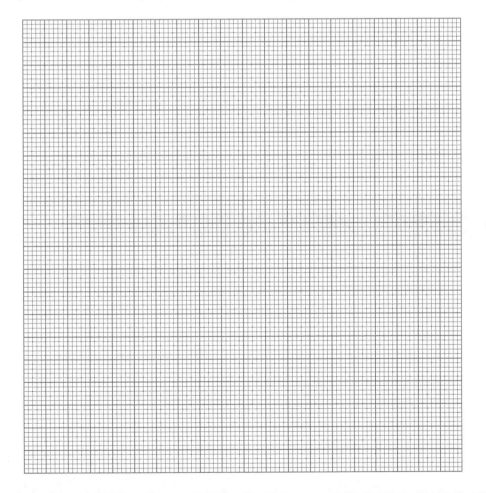

Analysis

3 Comment on the relationship between current and p.d. Use your graph to support your answer.

....

....

....

4 A student conducts a similar investigation, using a different resistor, and when he plots his graph the gradient is steeper. Explain what this implies about the resistance of the resistor.

....

....

5 Resistors are known as 'ohmic conductors'. Looking at the relationship between current and p.d. in your results, try to define the term 'ohmic conductor'.

....

....

....

Evaluation

6 One way to improve reliability is to repeat results and take an average. Suggest one other way to improve reliability in this investigation.

....

....

REFLECTION

A zero error occurs when a measuring device has a reading, even when it is not in the circuit. With a partner, discuss how you would adapt your readings if your ammeter had a zero error.

EXAM-STYLE QUESTIONS

1   A student is asked to determine the resistance of some unknown resistors.
    He set up the circuit shown.

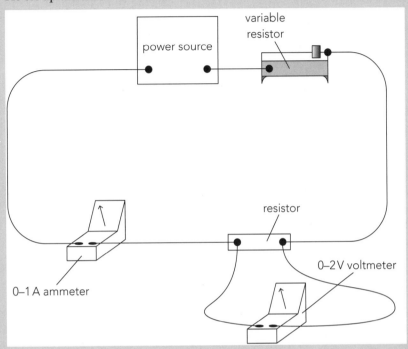

He measured the current, *I* and the potential difference, *V* across each resistor.
The readings are shown in the table.

V	I	R ....
2.00	0.080	
1.40	0.034	
2.00	0.024	
1.20	0.012	

a   i   Add the relevant units to each of the headings in the table.   [1]

    ii **Calculate** the resistance of each of the resistors and add them
        to the table.   [4]

COMMAND WORD

calculate: work out
from given facts,
figures or information

CONTINUED

b **State** one safety precaution you would take if you were conducting this investigation. [1]

....

Another student is asked to investigate how the current in a wire changes as the voltage across it changes. She is supplied with:

- a variable power supply
- an ammeter
- a voltmeter
- a test piece of wire
- connecting leads.

c Draw a circuit diagram of the circuit this student would have to set up in order to conduct the investigation stated for the test wire. [3]

The student conducts the investigation and obtains these results.

V / V	I / A
2.00	0.08
4.00	0.17
6.00	0.24
8.00	0.30
10.00	0.39
12.00	0.49

CONTINUED

d i Use the results to plot a graph of $V/$V against $I/$A. [5]

ii The gradient of the line represents the resistance of the wire.
Calculate the resistance of the wire and provide the relevant units. [3]

....

....

....

iii A third student comments that the current is directly proportional
to the voltage. State whether or not this student is correct. **Give** a
reason for your answer. [2]

Correct / incorrect ....

Reason ....

[Total: 19]

COMMAND WORD

give: produce an
answer from a given
source or recall/
memory

CONTINUED

2 A student investigates the effects of temperature on a thermistor.
The student keeps the current through the thermistor constant but varies
the temperature between 5 °C and 80 °C.

He uses a cell, a variable resistor, an ammeter, a voltmeter and a thermistor.

a **Sketch** a circuit diagram for this experiment. [3]

COMMAND WORDS

sketch: make a simple freehand drawing showing the key features, taking care over proportions

suggest: apply knowledge and understanding to situations where there are a range of valid responses in order to make proposals / put forward considerations

The thermistor is placed in a water bath to vary its temperature.
A thermometer is placed in the water bath to measure the temperature.

b **Suggest** two things the student must do to ensure that his temperature
readings are accurate. [2]

....

....

c i State the equation linking current, voltage and resistance. [1]

....

ii At 25 °C the current measured through the thermistor is 10 mA.
The potential difference across the thermistor is 6 V. Calculate the
resistance of the thermistor. Give the relevant unit. [4]

....

....

....

....

[Total: 10]

> Chapter 19
Electric circuits

THE INVESTIGATIONS IN THIS CHAPTER WILL:

- allow you to investigate the differences between series and parallel circuits and understand why parallel circuits are used instead of series circuits for electrical sockets in a house
- allow you to investigate the role of thermistors in circuits, which can be used to trigger heat sensing fire alarms.
- allow you to investigate what happens in circuits when the current surges and explain how safety devices such as fuses protect users.

Practical investigation 19.1: Light-dependent resistors

KEY WORDS

intensity: the power of the light over a certain area – brighter lights are more intense
lux: the unit of measurement for intensity
ohmmeter: a device used to measure the resistance of a component in a circuit

IN THIS INVESTIGATION YOU WILL:

- construct circuits containing a light-dependent resistor.

YOU WILL NEED:

- ohmmeter (or an ammeter in series to the LDR and a voltmeter in parallel to the LDR)
- 12 V lamp • metre ruler • connecting wires • power supply • black card
- light-dependent resistor (LDR)

Safety

Turn off the lamp when it is not in use to prevent overheating and to reduce the risk of burns.

Getting started

It can be tricky to block out all external light. The 'Method' section suggests using a funnel of black card to do this.

Look at the materials you have available to you. Could you create something better to help block out the light?

Look around the room. Where is the best place for the experiment? Do you need to consider anything about your surroundings that might affect how much external light reaches the LDR?

Write down your considerations.

....

....

....

....

Method

1   Set up the circuits as shown in Figure 19.1.

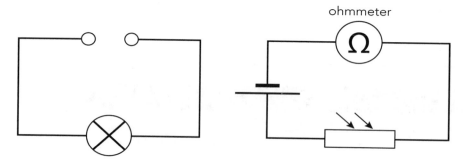

Figure 19.1: Circuit with bulb and circuit with ohmmeter.

2   Wrap the black card around the light to form a funnel.

3   Turn on the power supply so that the lamp is acting as the light source.

4   Connect the ohmmeter to the LDR.

5   Choose suitable distances from the lamp at which to position the LDR.

6   Record the resistance of the LDR at these positions.

Recording data

1   Record your results in the table.

Distance from the light source / cm	Resistance / Ω

> **TIP**
>
> You should aim to take at least six measurements to ensure a good range in your graph.

Handling data

2   Plot a graph of resistance against distance from the light source.

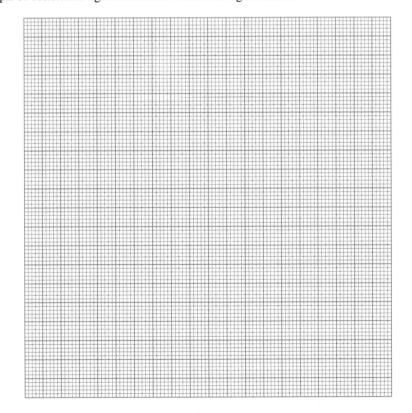

Analysis

3 Looking at your results, what can you conclude about the relationship between light intensity and resistance in an LDR? Use your results to support your answer.

....

....

....

4 Is it possible to use this LDR in a circuit that turns on a light when the light intensity is low? Give a reason for your answer.

....

....

....

Evaluation

5 An LDR's resistance depends on the intensity of light to which it is exposed. Describe one way in which you reduced the potential error due to exposure to background light.

....

....

....

....

6 Suggest how the experimental method could be changed so that the light intensity in lux is measured rather than the distance from the lamp.

....

....

....

....

....

Practical investigation 19.2: Thermistors

IN THIS INVESTIGATION YOU WILL:

- design an investigation to determine the relationship between temperature and resistance in a thermistor
- create circuits containing thermistors.

YOU WILL NEED:

- thermistor • beaker • hot water • small plastic bag • ....
- .... • ....

Safety

In this investigation you will be using hot water to alter the temperature of the thermistor. Write down two safety precautions you will need to take for this investigation.

- ....

- ....

Getting started

Using your knowledge of how temperature affects resistance, discuss with a partner how you think the temperature will affect the resistance of a thermistor. Write down your thoughts here.

....

....

....

....

State the dependent and independent variables in this investigation.

Dependent variable (the one you measure) ....

Independent variable (the one you choose) ....

Method

Write a method for your investigation. You should:

- complete the 'You will need' list
- draw a circuit diagram
- reference the dependent, independent and control variables and how you will measure and control them
- write a description of how you will conduct the investigation.

....

....

....

....

....

....

Recording data

1   You will need to tabulate your data for this investigation. Draw your table of results in the space below.

Handling data

2   Plot a graph of resistance (vertical axis) against temperature (horizontal axis).

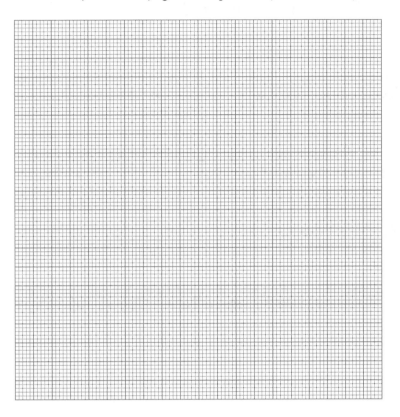

Analysis

3   Using your graph as justification, explain the relationship between temperature and resistance in a thermistor.

   ....

   ....

Evaluation

4   List two ways in which you ensured accurate readings in this investigation.

   ....

REFLECTION

- Do you think the method you wrote truly reflected the way you conducted the investigation? With a partner, discuss how you think your method could be improved.
- Go back to your method and make alterations in a different coloured pen.

Practical investigation 19.3: Investigating resistors in series and in parallel

Safety

- Turn the circuit off when it is not in use to prevent overheating of the resistors.
- Place a heatproof mat underneath the resistors to protect the workbench surface from overheating.

Getting started

Set up a basic series circuit including two lamps, a cell, an ammeter and a voltmeter. Ask a partner to check it for you.

Now re-organise your circuit so that the lamps are now in parallel. Your voltmeter should be positioned such that the voltmeter is reading the potential difference across the second lamp.

Ask your partner to check it for you to ensure you have connected up the circuit correctly.

Method

1   Set up a circuit as shown in Figure 19.2.

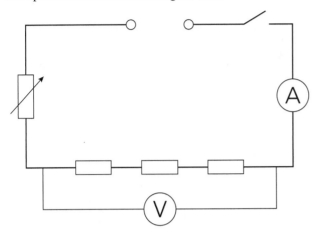

Figure 19.2: Circuit with voltmeter in parallel to three resistors.

2   Connect the voltmeter in parallel to the three resistors.

3   Turn the circuit on and record the potential difference across the resistors and current in the circuit. Record the values in the table. Repeat this step.

4   Using the variable resistor, alter the current in the circuit. Record results for three more readings of V and I.

5   Disconnect the circuit. Now set up a circuit with the three resistors in parallel. Position the ammeter so that it measures the current before the first junction and place the voltmeter so that it measures the p.d. across the resistors connected in parallel.

> **TIP**
>
> Build a basic series loop first with one resistor. Connect the remaining resistors with wires connected to the terminals of the first resistor.

6   Measure the total current through the circuit and the potential difference across the resistors connected in parallel. Record the values in the table. Repeat this step.

7   Change the current in the circuit using the variable resistor. Record readings for V and I for three more values of V.

Recording data

1   Record your results in the tables below.

Potential difference / V			Current / A			Resistance / Ω
1	2	Average	1	2	Average	

Three resistors connected in series

Potential difference / V			Current / A			Resistance / Ω
1	2	Average	1	2	Average	

Three resistors connected in parallel

2   Draw a circuit diagram for the second circuit you connected in this investigation in the space below.

Handling data

3   Calculate the average values for potential difference and current for both combinations of resistors and record in the tables above.

4   Calculate the resistance for both combinations of resistors and record in the tables above.

....

....

....

....

....

Analysis

5   Compare the resistances of both combinations of resistors. What can you conclude from this investigation? Use your results to support your answer.

....

....

....

....

....

Evaluation

6   State one precaution you took in this experiment to ensure reliable results were obtained and give a reason for your answer.

....

....

....

....

....

Practical investigation 19.4: Investigating fuses

IN THIS INVESTIGATION YOU WILL:

- select and use appropriate trip switches and fuses in circuits
- understand that fuses protect circuits and cables in domestic appliances.

YOU WILL NEED:

- six lamps • ammeter • three 1.5 V cells • component holder
- crocodile clips • leads • variable resistor • cartridge fuse of 0.25 A

Safety

Turn off the circuit when not in use to prevent it from overheating.

Method

1 Set up the circuit as shown in Figure 19.3 but start with just two lamps in series.

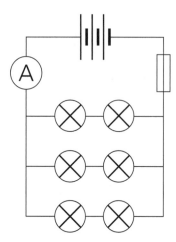

Figure 19.3: Circuit diagram with three sets of two lamps in parallel.

> **TIP**
>
> Build a basic series loop first with one resistor. Connect the remaining resistors with wires connected to the terminals of the first resistor.

2 Record the current in the table.

3 Add another pair of lamps in parallel to the first set. Record the current in the table.

4   Repeat step **3**.

5   Set up a new circuit as in Figure 19.4.

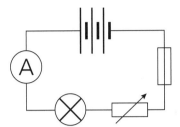

Figure 19.4: Circuit diagram with ammeter, lamp and resistor in series.

6   Slowly reduce the resistance in the circuit, using the variable resistor.

7   Note the current reading at which the fuse blows.

Recording data

1   Record your results in the table.

Number of lamps	Current / A

2   State the current reading at which the fuse blows.

....

Analysis

3   In the first circuit why did the fuse not blow? Give reasoning for your answer.

....

....

....

4   Looking at your results, do you think the rating on the fuse is correct? Provide reasoning for your answer.

....

....

Evaluation

5 Explain why a variable resistor, rather than a 1 V step power pack, was used in the circuit.

....

....

6 In this investigation did you use a digital or analogue ammeter? Discuss with a partner why a digital ammeter might be better to use than an analogue ammeter. Can you think of a benefit for using an analogue over a digital meter?

....

....

REFLECTION

Consider your investigation and the method you used. With a partner discuss one of the errors that could have occurred in the investigation and suggest a way in which this could be reduced.

EXAM-STYLE QUESTIONS

1 A student is asked to investigate the total resistance of three components
   when they are arranged differently into two electrical circuits. The circuits
   are shown below.

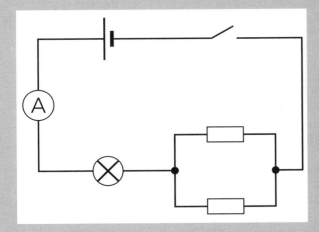

Circuit 1

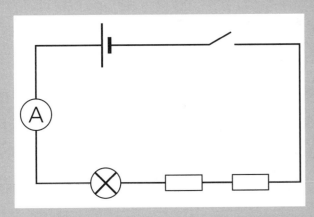

Circuit 2

a Add a voltmeter to the circuit to measure the voltage across all of
   the components in both circuits.   [1]

   When the switch is closed the student records the voltmeter and
   ammeter reading in this table.

Circuit	V/...	I/...	Total resistance in the circuit/........	Appearance of the lamp
1	1.49	0.50		
2	1.48	0.22		

b Fill in the missing units for the column which is missing units.   [2]

CONTINUED

c i State the equation linking resistance, voltage and current. [1]

....

ii Use the equation to calculate the total resistance in each of the circuits. [2]

....

d Predict the appearance of the lamp in each of the circuits. [2]

....

....

e A student suggests that to reduce the resistance in the circuits you could add in another resistor. State whether you agree with the statement and give reasoning for your answer. [2]

....

....

[Total: 10]

COMMAND WORDS

state: express in clear terms

predict: suggest what may happen based on available information

Electromagnetic forces

- allow you to investigate the magnetic effects of a current flowing through a circuit and appreciate the safety features of a relay circuit in everyday uses

- allow you to investigate the force on a current-carrying conductor; for example, this technology can be used to create motors for use in cars, or even a standard home hairdryer

- allow you to investigate the factors that affect the speed of a motor, knowledge that enables engineers to increase the power output of cars.

Practical investigation 20.1: Making a relay circuit

KEY WORD

relay circuit: a low-power circuit that is used as a safety feature to turn on a higher-power circuit

IN THIS INVESTIGATION YOU WILL:

- build a circuit with a relay and understand the principles behind it.

YOU WILL NEED:

- insulated copper wire • connecting leads • laminated C-core • 1.5 V cell • switch
- steel strip • clamp and two wooden blocks • 12 V power supply • 12 V lamp • tape

Safety

Ensure that the steel strips are not magnetic before using them.

Getting started

How will you test to ensure that the steel strips and the C-core are not magnetic before use?

....

....

Method

1   Wind the copper wire around the C-core approximately 20 times and attach one end to the 1.5 V cell.

2   Connect the other free end of the wire to the switch and connect the switch to the other end of the cell via a connecting lead.

3   Clamp one end of the steel strip and place the C-core underneath so that the strip is close to but not quite touching the C-core.

4   Tape some insulated copper wire along the length of the steel strip (see Figure 20.1). Allow a few centimetres of the wire to overhang the end that is furthest from the clamp.

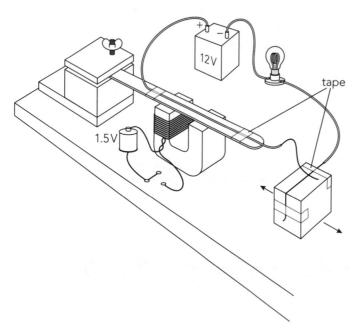

Figure 20.1: Experimental set-up for a relay circuit.

5   Connect the end of the insulated copper wire that is nearer the clamp to a 12 V cell or power supply.

6   Expose approximately 2 cm of the insulated copper wire overhanging the free end of the steel strip and bend it into a hill shape.

7   Underneath the free end of the wire, position a wooden block. Remove about 2 cm of insulation from one end of another piece of copper wire and tape it onto the wooden block. Attach the other end of this wire to one terminal of a 12 V lamp.

8   Attach another wire from the free terminal of the lamp to the 12 V cell to complete the circuit (see Figure 20.1).

TIP
Make sure the C-core is near enough to attract the steel strip when it is magnetised.

Recording data

1   Explain what you notice about the lamp in the 12 V circuit when the switch is *open* on the 1.5 V cell.

....

....

....

2   Explain what you notice about the lamp in the 12 V circuit when the switch is *closed* on the 1.5 V cell.

....

....

....

Analysis

3   Explain how to use the smaller 1.5 V circuit to turn on the 12 V circuit.

....

....

....

4   Relay circuits are often used as safety measures. Explain why using a relay circuit is safer than just turning on the 12 V circuit directly.

....

....

....

Evaluation

5   Explain why a magnetic material, rather than a non-magnetic material, would need to be used for the strip.

....

....

....

6 Another student builds the same relay circuit, but struggles to get it to work because the magnetic field of the C-core is not strong enough. Suggest one way in which the student could increase the strength of the C-core's magnetic field.

....

....

REFLECTION

- This circuit can sometimes be tricky to get working the first time you build it. In the space provided, write down all the things you did to overcome any issues in setting up the circuit.

    ....

    ....

- Remember to use these solutions when you next face a problem in an electrical circuit.

Practical investigation 20.2: The motor effect

KEY WORD

electric motor: a device that transfers electrical and magnetic energy into kinetic energy

---

IN THIS INVESTIGATION YOU WILL:

- build a simple electric motor and determine what causes a change in speed and direction.

YOU WILL NEED:

- four circular disc magnets • tape • board • compass • crocodile clips
- a length of insulated copper wire • two 1.5 V batteries connected with leads

---

Safety

- Only connect the circuit when you are observing it, to prevent overheating.

- When handling the magnets, take care not to trap your fingers when they come together.

Getting started

Draw the magnetic field lines around the magnets in the diagram.

If you were to 'cut' these field lines with a wire, what would be the angle between the wire and the field?

....

....

....

Method

1   Fit the disc magnets together so that their opposing poles are aligned and they form a cylinder shape (see Figure 20.2).

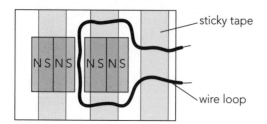

Figure 20.2: Disc magnets aligned in a cylinder shape.

2   Split the cylinder in half, leaving a 1 cm gap between the discs and tape to the board.

3   Use the compass to mark on the board the direction of the magnetic field in the gap between the magnets.

4   Place the wire in the gap and bend it around and away from one stack of the magnets.

5   Strip 1 cm of insulation off each end of the wire and connect it to the batteries, using crocodile clips. Record your observations.

6   Swap the ends of the wire to the opposite terminals and place the wire in the magnetic field again. Record your observations.

Recording data

1   What did you observe when the wire was placed inside the magnetic field and the circuit was turned on?

....

....

2   When the direction of the current was reversed, what effect did this have on the movement of the copper wire?

....

....

3   Suggest how reversing the field of the magnets will affect the movement of the wire.

....

> TIP
>
> Consider what happened when you reversed the polarity of the current.

Evaluation

4 Copper conducts electricity. Why are fibreglass wires not suitable?

....

....

5 Another student conducts this investigation but finds that the movement of the wire is very small. How can they adapt their circuit to increase the movement observed?

....

....

EXAM-STYLE QUESTIONS

1 A student is asked to demonstrate the motor effect. He is given the apparatus shown.

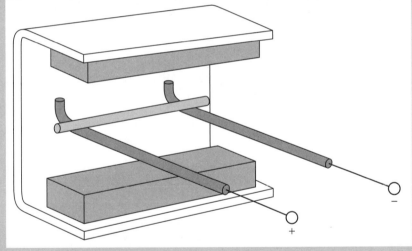

a On the diagram, label:

    copper rod   magnets   direction of current   **[2]**

b i The student turns the circuit on. **Suggest** what he will observe.   **[2]**

    ....

    ....

COMMAND WORD

suggest: apply knowledge and understanding to situations where there are a range of valid responses in order to make proposals / put forward considerations

CONTINUED

ii The student reverses the direction of the current.
Suggest what he will observe this time. **[2]**

....

....

c i Suggest two ways in which the student could increase the movement
of the copper rod. **[2]**

....

....

....

....

ii Suggest one reason why the student used a copper rod rather
than another material. **[1]**

....

[Total: 9]

> Chapter 21
Electromagnetic induction

THE INVESTIGATIONS IN THIS CHAPTER WILL:

- allow you to investigate the factors affecting the strength of the e.m.f. produced in electromagnetic induction so that we are able to increase electricity supply

- allow you to discover how a.c. generators are made from the basic principles of electromagnetic induction for devices such as a wind up torch

- allow you to discover the relationship between the number of coils and the type of transformer created, which is useful for understanding how transformers can be used to decrease or increase our everyday electricity supply.

Practical investigation 21.1: Electromagnetic induction in a coil

KEY WORDS

e.m.f. (electromotive force): the electrical work done by a source (cell, battery etc.) in moving (a unit) charge around a circuit

galvanometer: an ammeter that detects small changes in current

generate: to create

infrared radiation: an electromagnetic wave that is just beyond the red end of the visible spectrum

IN THIS INVESTIGATION YOU WILL:

- carry out an experiment to demonstrate electromagnetic induction
- determine the factors that affect an induced e.m.f.

YOU WILL NEED:

- insulated copper wire • cardboard tube • tape • galvanometer • bar magnet

Safety

Separate bar magnets with caution to avoid pinching your skin between them.

> Getting started

Look at the galvanometer readings on the four meters. Practise reading the scale and write the value below each one.

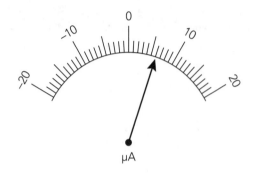

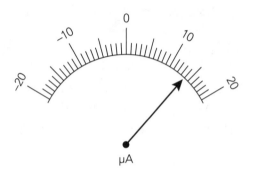

....

....

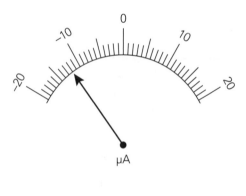

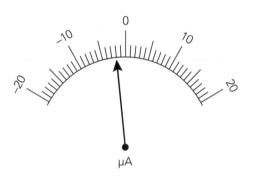

....

....

Method

1   Coil the copper wire tightly around the kitchen roll tube 75 times and tape it into place.

2   Expose 2 cm of the copper wire at either end and attach to the terminals of the galvanometer.

3   Push the magnet inside the coil and tube and record the maximum reading on the galvanometer.

4   Remove the magnet from the coil and record the reading on the galvanometer.

5   Place the magnet inside the tube and record your observations.

> **TIP**
>
> If the galvanometer barely moves, use iron wool on the exposed ends of the wire to remove any dirt or coating and hence reduce the resistance between the contacts.

Recording data

1   Describe your observations and record any readings on the galvanometer that you observed as you *pushed* the magnet inside the coil of wire.

   ....

   ....

   ....

2   Describe your observations and record any readings on the galvanometer that you observed as you *removed* the magnet from inside the coil of wire.

   ....

   ....

   ....

3   Describe your observations and record any readings on the galvanometer that you observed when the magnet remains *stationary* inside the coil of wire.

   ....

   ....

   ....

4   Increase the number of turns on the coil. Describe your observations and record any readings on the galvanometer that you observed when the magnet *went in and out* of the coil of wire.

   ....

   ....

   ....

5   Change the speed at which the magnet is pushed in and out of the wire. Describe what you notice, compared to when you pushed the magnet inside the coil in question **4**.

   ....

   ....

   ....

Analysis

6   Review your observations and write a conclusion about the relationship between the number of turns on the wire and the size of electromotive force (e.m.f.) generated and therefore the current induced in the wire.

....

....

....

7   Write a conclusion about the relationship between the speed of movement and the size of e.m.f. generated, and therefore the current induced, in the wire.

....

....

....

Evaluation

8   Another student wants to conduct a more detailed investigation on the relationship between the number of coils on the wire and the size of current induced. Identify the dependent and independent variables.

....

....

....

9   State one control variable for the student's investigation and suggest one way to ensure it does not affect the results.

....

....

....

10 Explain why a two-way galvanometer, rather than an ammeter, might be used in this investigation.

....

....

....

Practical investigation 21.2: Investigating transformers

KEY WORDS

generator: a device that transfers kinetic energy into electrical energy

iron yoke: a small iron bar used to create a closed iron square

transformer: a device that increases or decreases the voltage across it

IN THIS INVESTIGATION YOU WILL:

- describe how a simple transformer is constructed
- understand the terms primary, secondary, step-up and step-down in relation to transformers
- describe how transformers are used in the high voltage transmission of electricity.

YOU WILL NEED:

- transformer with detachable iron yoke • 4 m insulated copper wire
- wire coil of 1200 turns • 2.5 V bulb with holder

Safety

The primary coil may overheat if it is left on for too long. Turn off the transformer when it is not in use to reduce the risk of burns.

Getting started

Label all of the key components in a transformer, and describe their role, on the diagram. You may wish to use a real transformer for reference.

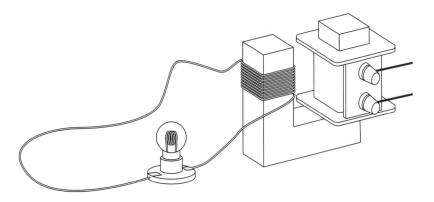

Method

Your teacher will set up the transformer, as shown in Figure 21.1.

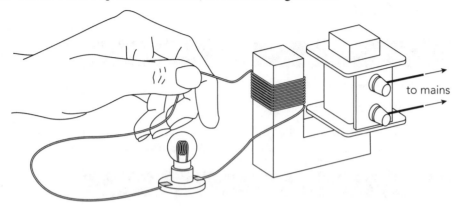

Figure 21.1: A simple transformer.

The primary coil has 1200 turns of copper wire and is connected to the mains supply (230 V a.c.). The secondary coil is connected to a 9 V bulb. During the investigation you will record your observations as the number of turns on the secondary coil increases.

Recording data

1   There are 1200 turns on the primary coil of the transformer. Your teacher will add a secondary coil of 20 turns. Record your observations. Refer to the brightness of the lamp and any other observations you make.

....

....

2   Predict what you think will happen to the brightness of the lamp when another 20 turns are added to the secondary coil.

....

....

3   Your teacher will now add another 20 turns to the coil. Describe the brightness of the lamp in comparison to its brightness when there were only 20 turns.

....

....

4   Do these observations support your prediction?

....

....

5   Your teacher will now add the top part of the iron core to the transformer (the yoke).
    Predict what you think will happen to the brightness of the lamp. Give a reason for your answer.

    ....

    ....

    ....

6   Do your observations support your prediction? If not explain why.

    ....

    ....

Analysis

7   There are two types of transformer: step-up transformers and step-down transformers. With
    reference to your observations, which type do you think was demonstrated in this practical?

    ....

    ....

Evaluation

8   With a partner, discuss one way in which the investigation could be altered to allow for
    numerical data to be obtained to support your observations. Make a note of anything
    you could do in the space provided.

    ....

    ....

REFLECTION

•   Consider the structure of the transformer. Discuss why the transformer vibrates when a
    magnetic field is oscillating in the yoke.

•   How is the structure of the transformer adapted to try and reduce these vibrations?

EXAM-STYLE QUESTIONS

1 A student is asked to construct a simple generator and investigate how the level of induced e.m.f. changes with the speed of rotation. The generator is set up as shown in the diagram below.

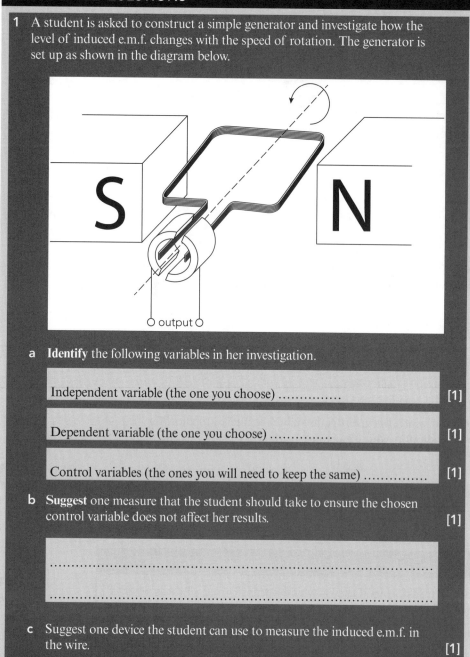

a **Identify** the following variables in her investigation.

Independent variable (the one you choose) .... [1]

Dependent variable (the one you choose) .... [1]

Control variables (the ones you will need to keep the same) .... [1]

b **Suggest** one measure that the student should take to ensure the chosen control variable does not affect her results. [1]

....

....

c Suggest one device the student can use to measure the induced e.m.f. in the wire. [1]

....

[Total: 5]

COMMAND WORDS

identify: name / select / recognise

suggest: apply knowledge and understanding to situations where there are a range of valid responses in order to make proposals / put forward considerations

Chapter 22

The nuclear atom

THE INVESTIGATIONS IN THIS CHAPTER WILL:

- allow you to describe the composition of the atom and challenge historical ideas of the different atomic models
- allow you to define the composition of the nucleus and illustrate isotopes of different elements, which are fundamental when determining the age of artefacts in archaeology.

Practical investigation 22.1: The structure of the atom

KEY WORDS

adapt: to change something

isotope: an atom of an element that contains the same number of protons but differing numbers of neutrons

simulation: a computer model of what happens in the real situation

IN THIS INVESTIGATION YOU WILL:

- describe and model the structure of an atom
- adapt an atom model to show isotopes and explain what they are.

YOU WILL NEED:

- ten red beads (protons)   • ten blue beads (neutrons)   • ten white beads (electrons)
- paper plate   • string (optional)

Getting started

In the space provided, make notes about the key information about the following parts of an atom:

Protons ....

Neutrons ....

Electrons ....

Method

1 Collect the beads and a paper plate.

2 Arrange the beads as they would be found in an atom of $^{14}_{7}N$, $^{12}_{6}C$, $^{4}_{2}He$ and $^{7}_{3}Li$.

Recording data

1 Sketch the atoms you have created.

2 Adapt your models to illustrate an isotope of each of the elements $^{14}_{7}N$, $^{12}_{6}C$, $^{4}_{2}He$ and $^{7}_{3}Li$. Sketch these isotopes.

Analysis

3 Explain how this model represents the structure of the atom.

....

....

....

....

4 Suggest two similarities and two differences between this model and the real structure of an atom.

....

....

....

....

Evaluation

5 Suggest one way in which you could amend this model to make it a more accurate representation of the atom.

....

....

6 Why might the Solar System provide a better representation of the atom than this model?

....

....

Practical investigation 22.2: The alpha scattering experiment

IN THIS INVESTIGATION YOU WILL:

> model the scattering of alpha (α-) particles.

YOU WILL NEED:

- nine 2-litre drinks bottles (or small drinks bottles) • table tennis balls (or marbles)

Safety

Marbles can be a slip hazard. Ensure they are kept safely in a box before and after the modelling activity.

Getting started

Place the bottles in the following arrangements. Roll one ball to the arrangement and write down what you think what would happen if you were to continue rolling balls at them.

In a circle with all bottles touching:

....

In a diamond shape with all bottles touching:

....

In a circle with bottles touching sides and a space in the middle:

....

In a square with no spaces between bottles:

....

Method

1   Arrange the drinks bottles in a regular lattice formation, 1 m apart from each other, as in Figure 22.1.

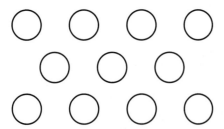

Figure 22.1: Regular lattice formation.

2   Roll the table tennis balls towards the bottles, from different positions. Note whether the balls pass through, collide and deflect or collide and rebound in each case.

3   Repeat until at least 20 table tennis balls have passed through.

Recording data

1   A model is often used as a way to describe what is happening in situations when it is not easy physically to see what is occurring. Describe what each of the components in this model represents.

Table tennis balls   ....

Drinks bottles   ....

2   Roll a table tennis ball directly towards the centre of a drinks bottle. Describe the path of the ball before and after it strikes the bottle.

....

....

TIP
Roll the ball with greater force to see a greater deflection.

3   Align the table tennis ball so that it will now strike towards the edge of a bottle. Describe the path of the ball before and after it strikes the bottle.

....

....

4   Describe how altering the alignment of your roll relative to a bottle affects the deflection observed.

....

....

Analysis

5   Explain why the tennis ball deflects 180° when it is rolled directly towards the bottle.

....

....

6   Why would this deflection occur infrequently in Rutherford's scattering experiment?

....

....

Evaluation

7   Models can be a useful way of representing what is happening in situations that are not easily visible. Compare and suggest two similarities between Rutherford's scattering and this model investigation.

....

....

REFLECTION

- Modelling is often used to show difficult concepts that cannot be observed easily. This means that whilst they have great similarities, there can also be differences, which means the model does not work exactly as the situation would. Discuss with a partner and suggest two differences between Rutherford's scattering experiment and this model investigation.

  ....

  ....

- Make two suggestions on how this model investigation could be improved to make the results more consistent with the Rutherford scattering results.

  ....

  ....

EXAM-STYLE QUESTIONS

1   A student is discussing the different isotopes of Nitrogen. He discovers that the most abundant isotope in the atmosphere is $^{14}_{7}N$.

a   For a neutral atom of this isotope state:

  i   The proton number ....

  ii   The nucleon number ....

  iii   The number of neutrons ....

  iv   The number of electrons ....

b   In 1911 Ernst Rutherford fired a beam of alpha particles at a thin sheet of gold in a vacuum. It was found that the majority of particles passed straight through the foil. Some however were deflected and a very small proportion rebounded completely.

  i   Considering the charge on an alpha particle, **explain** what this would suggest about the nucleus of an atom.

....

....

....

....

  ii   **State** what two conclusions can be drawn about the nuclei of atoms based on this experiment.

  1   ....

  2   ....

COMMAND WORDS

explain: set out purposes or reasons / make the relationships between things evident / provide why and/or how and support with relevant evidence

state: express in clear terms

> ## Chapter 23
Radioactivity

THE INVESTIGATIONS IN THIS CHAPTER WILL:

- allow you to explore radioactive decay, which is integral to selecting the correct radioisotopes for use in medicine and industry

- allow you to determine the half-life of an isotope, which enables scientists to date ancient artefacts.

Practical investigation 23.1: Radioactive decay model

KEY WORDS

decay: when an atom changes into another element by releasing radiation

half-life: the time it takes for the activity of a radioactive sample to halve

model: a situation that acts or behaves in a similar way to scientific principle

IN THIS INVESTIGATION YOU WILL:

- model radioactive decay of isotopes

- calculate half-life from a decay curve.

YOU WILL NEED:

- 25 six-sided spinners   • tray

Getting started

Take a piece of paper and cut it in half. Now take this new piece and cut it in half again. Repeat this until you can cut it no longer.

Now imagine the paper was a sample. Each time you cut the paper in half, you are halving the number of radioactive isotopes in the sample.

In this investigation you will be modelling what happens to get to that halfway point and representing the random way in which this occurs in a graph.

Method

In this model, the spinners represent undecayed nuclei. Every time you spin the spinner and it lands on a 6, one nuclei has decayed. This represents the random nature of the decay.

1   Spin all 25 spinners in the tray.

2   Remove from the tray any spinners that have landed with a 6 upwards. Count the remaining spinners and record this number in the table of results.

3   Repeat the process again until you have no spinners left.

Recording data

1   Draw your table of results in the space below. The headings have been completed for you.

Number of rolls (time)	Remaining spinners (undecayed nuclei)

Handling data

2   Plot your results on the axes provided. The number of spins represents the time and should be plotted along the horizontal axis. The remaining spinners after each spin represent the undecayed nuclei and should be plotted on the vertical axis.

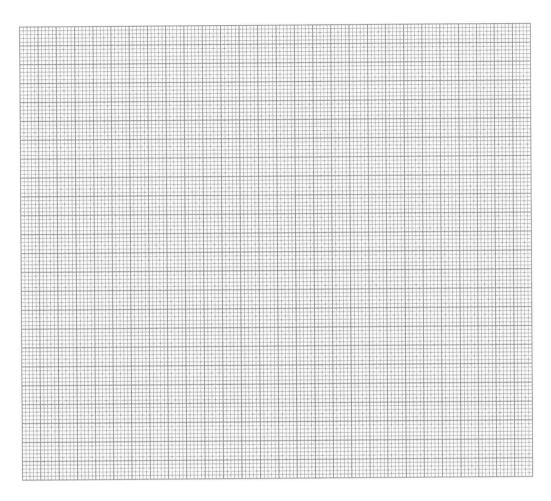

Analysis

3   Draw a curve of best fit to show the trend in the decay of the nuclei.

> **TIP**
>
> It can be difficult to draw a smooth curve. Rotate the page so that the arc of your forearm follows the curvature of the pattern. This will make it easier to draw.

4   Determine the half-life of the spinners for this model.

....

5   Compare this with another group's data. Are the half-lives similar?
Give a reason for your answer.

....

....

6 How many spinners would be left after two half-lives?

....

Evaluation

7 If you doubled the sample size to 50 spinners, do you think that the half-life would change? Give a reason for your answer.

....

....

....

8 Models are used to convey scientific ideas that might be tricky to understand. Describe the ways in which this model investigation is similar to real-life radioactive decay.

....

....

9 Describe the ways in which this model is different to real-life radioactive decay.

....

....

10 Do you think this is an appropriate model for radioactive decay? Suggest a different model that could be used instead.

....

....

REFLECTION

Look back at this investigation with a partner. Discuss how you think your understanding of a random event has changed. Use the results to support your discussion.

EXAM-STYLE QUESTIONS

1 A student has been asked to investigate the amount of beta (β)-particles that pass through different thicknesses of aluminium. She uses a Geiger–Müller tube to record the amount of nuclei that passes each second. The apparatus is set up as shown.

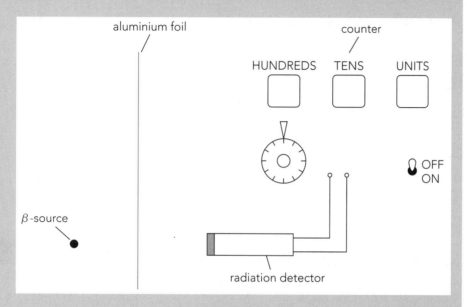

The detector is turned on for 3 minutes with no source present. After this time, the counter reads:

a i The Geiger–Müller tube is detecting background radiation.
   Calculate the average count rate of this radiation, in counts/minute.   [2]

   ....

   ....

ii Suggest two sources for this background radiation.   [2]

   ....

   ....

Before conducting the investigation, the student reads the safety precautions for handling radioactive sources in the school safety handbook.

COMMAND WORDS

calculate: work out from given facts, figures or information

suggest: apply knowledge and understanding to situations where there are a range of valid responses in order to make proposals / put forward considerations

CONTINUED

b Suggest two safety considerations the student might read in the booklet.

i .... [1]

ii .... [1]

The student goes on to conduct the investigation and her results are shown in the table.

Aluminium sheet thickness / mm	Count rate / counts/minute
2	561
5	288
10	152
15	92
20	56

c i **Describe** the relationship between the amount of β-particles that pass through aluminium and the sheet's thickness.
Give justification for your answer. [2]

....

....

....

ii **State** one control variable for this investigation. [1]

....

The student worries the results are not reliable.

d Suggest one way in which she could increase the reliability of her results. [1]

....

....

[Total: 10]

COMMAND WORDS

describe: state the points of a topic / give characteristics and main features

give: produce an answer from a given source or recall/ memory

state: express in clear terms

Chapter 24
Earth and the Solar System

THE INVESTIGATIONS IN THIS CHAPTER WILL:

- allow you to determine the phases of the Moon using a model. Models are used by scientists when they cannot take real measurements due to restrictions in size of the matter or ability to see the situation.

Practical investigation 24.1:
Phases of the Moon

KEY WORD

phase: a period of time or a stage in the Moon's motion

IN THIS INVESTIGATION YOU WILL:

- use a model to make observations of the Moon's phases
- draw conclusions from your observations about the Moon's position during its motion around the earth.

YOU WILL NEED:

- a tall lamp • a tennis ball or ball of similar size • a darkened room

Safety

- Remove trip hazards before conducting the investigation.
- Once the room is darkened stay in your position in the room.

Getting started

In this investigation, the way you hold the ball will be important.

Pick up the tennis ball and hold it in the air, out in front of you, above your head. Turn your back to the lamp and practise positioning your hand and your body so that you are not blocking the light from the lamp.

What does the lamp in this model represent?

....

What does the ball represent?

....

Method

1   Place the tall lamp in the centre of the room and switch it on.

2   Darken the room so the only light that you can see is from the tall lamp.

3   Raise the tennis ball and hold it in the air, out in front of you, at 45 degrees from the horizontal. Hold it so that there is no shadow cast on the ball. This is your starting position.

4   Now, staying on the same spot, turn 45 degrees anticlockwise. Note down your observations of how the light on the ball looks, in the table provided in the Recording data section.

5   Repeat steps 4 and 5 until you have completed one complete circle on the spot.

Recording data

1   Record your findings in the table.

Point from starting position	Sketch observation of the ball	Phase of the Moon
At start		
$\frac{1}{8}$ turn anticlockwise		
$\frac{1}{4}$ turn anticlockwise		
$\frac{3}{8}$ turn anticlockwise		
$\frac{1}{2}$ way through cycle		
$\frac{5}{8}$ turn anticlockwise		
$\frac{3}{4}$ turn anticlockwise		
$\frac{7}{8}$ turn anticlockwise		
Back to starting position		

Handling data

2 Determine the phase of the Moon represented for each position of the tennis ball. Record it in the table.

Analysis

3 How is the shape of a crescent Moon created in this model?

....

....

4 Some people suggest that the new Moon occurs because it is not visible. Explain why the new Moon is not visible to people on earth.

....

....

Evaluation

5 Suggest one way in which you could have improved this model of the phases of the Moon.

....

....

6 Suggest one way in which you could have demonstrated a solar eclipse using this model.

....

....

REFLECTION

With a partner, discuss how you managed to ensure your hand did not obscure the tennis ball shadow.

EXAM-STYLE QUESTIONS

1   A student is studying the night sky for a project.

He plans to take photographs of the Moon every 7 days, starting from the full Moon.

a   Complete the sketches of what the student would expect to see on the days listed below and the name of the phase of the Moon.

Day	Sketch	Phase of the Moon
1		Full Moon
7		
14		New Moon
21		
28		

[6]

b   The Moon takes approximately 28 days to orbit the Earth. The radius of the Moon's orbit is approximately 3.5×10^8 m.

   i   **State** the equation linking orbital speed, time period, and orbital radius.   [1]

   ii **Calculate** the orbital speed of the Moon in km/s.   [4]

c   **Explain** how the orbit of a comet is different to that of the Moon around the Earth.   [3]

COMMAND WORDS

state: express in clear terms

calculate: work out from given facts, figures or information

explain: set out purposes or reasons / make the relationships between things evident / provide why and/or how and support with relevant evidence

Chapter 25

Stars and the Universe

THE INVESTIGATIONS IN THIS CHAPTER WILL:

- allow you to calculate the gravitational field strength on earth and compare it to other planets. Such calculations help us to model how we could live on other planets and the effects that gravity may have on our bodies there.

Practical investigation 25.1: Determining the acceleration of free fall

KEY WORD

data logger: an instrument that records data at regular intervals

KEY EQUATION

$$\text{speed} = \frac{\text{distance travelled}}{\text{time}}$$

IN THIS INVESTIGATION YOU WILL:

- estimate the acceleration of free fall, as a consequence of the gravitational field on earth and compare it to the gravitational fields on planets of differing mass.

YOU WILL NEED:

- metre ruler • light gate • data logger and computer • two clamps • set square
- two metal stands • 10 cm square weighted piece of card with a line across it at 5 cm

Getting started

A light gate works by detecting when a light beam is broken, by a piece of card of known length, for a period of time. The length of time the light is broken for is recorded by the data logger.

Some data loggers can calculate the speed of a travelling object for you but others will only record the time.

Using the equation for speed, calculate the speed of the falling cards in the following situations. Remember to state the speed in m/s.

a A piece of card length 100 mm, time recorded 8 ms.

....

b A piece of card length 150 mm, time recorded 10 ms.

....

c A piece of card length 120 mm, time recorded 16 ms.

....

> **TIP**
>
> Remember 1 ms = 0.001 s, and 1 m = 0.001 mm.

Method

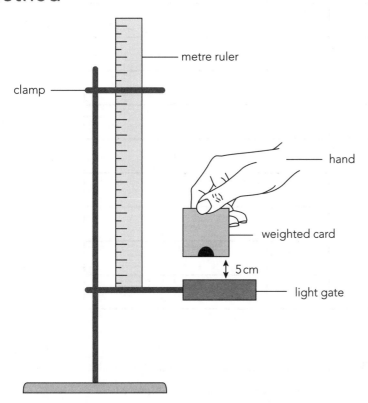

Figure 24.1: Acceleration of free fall experimental apparatus.

1 Set up the apparatus as shown in Figure 24.1. Clamp the light gate, which is connected to the data logger and computer, approximately 10 cm from the bench.

2 Using a set square, clamp the metre ruler vertically to the bench starting with 0 cm at the top of the light gate.

3 Line up the black line on the weighted card with the 5 cm mark on the ruler.

4 Release the card, ensuring it falls and breaks the light beam.

5 Record the time in the table.

6 Repeat steps **1–5** three times and calculate the average time taken for this height.

7 Repeat steps **1–6** with the card starting at a height of 10 cm, 15 cm, 20 cm, 25 cm, 30 cm, 35 cm, 40 cm, 45 cm and 50 cm.

Recording data

1 Record your results in the table.

Height of card drop, h / cm	Time recorded, t / ms				Speed of card, v / m/s	(Speed)^2, v^2
	1	2	3	Average		
5						
10						
15						
20						
25						
30						
35						
40						
45						
50						

Handling data

2 Calculate the speed of the card, v, through the light gate each time and record it in the table.

3 Calculate the (speed)^2, v^2, for each height of card drop and record it in the final column of the table.

4 Plot a graph on the grid on the next page of v^2 on the y-axis and the height of the card drop, h, on the x-axis.

5 Calculate the acceleration of free fall, which is equivalent to the gravitational field strength, from the gradient of your graph, using this equation:

acceleration of free fall (m/s^2) = gradient/2

....

....

....

Analysis

6 Looking at the shape of the graph, what can you determine about the relationship between v^2 and the height of the card drop, h?

....

....

....

7 Research the acceleration of free fall or gravitational field strength on Mercury, Mars, Saturn and Jupiter, and write their values in the space below.

....

....

....

8 Now compare your calculated value of acceleration of free fall on earth and your researched values for Mercury, Mars, Saturn and Jupiter, to the planet's respective masses. Comment on the pattern that you see and make a conclusion from the data you have.

....

....

....

Evaluation

9 Describe at least two sources for potential error in your measurements.

....

....

....

10 If you were to repeat this investigation, suggest two ways in which you could reduce these sources of error.

....

....

....

REFLECTION

- Discuss with a partner one of the biggest challenges you faced in taking the measurements in this investigation.

- Exchange ideas about how you could alter this investigation to take the measurements in a different way.

EXAM-STYLE QUESTIONS

1   A student is investigating the acceleration of free fall in an experiment.
    She measures the length of a pendulum and records the time taken for one
    oscillation. The results are shown in the table.

Length, l/m	Time, T/s	(Time)^2, T^2/s^2
0.1	0.63	
0.2	0.89	
0.3	1.10	
0.4	1.26	
0.5	1.41	
0.6	1.55	
0.7	1.67	

   a   Complete the final column in the table, T^2.   [2]

   b   Use the student's results to plot a graph of T^2 against length, l.   [2]

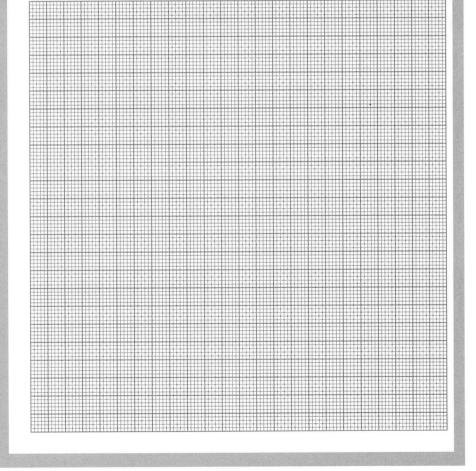

CONTINUED

c Draw a line of best fit on your graph. [1]

d From your line of best fit, **calculate** the gradient, G, of your line. [2]

....

....

e The student has only taken one reading per length in this investigation. **Explain** why the student should have taken more than one reading each time. [2]

....

....

f Explain a way in which the student could have reduced the effect of human error in her timing measurements. [2]

....

[Total: 11]

COMMAND WORDS

calculate: work out from given facts, figures or information

explain: set out purposes or reasons / make the relationships between things evident / provide why and/or how and support with relevant evidence

> Glossary

Command words

Below are the Cambridge International definitions for command words which may be used in exams. The information in this section is taken from the Cambridge International syllabus (0625/0972) for examination from 2023. You should always refer to the appropriate syllabus document for the year of your examination to confirm the details and for more information. The syllabus document is available on the Cambridge Assessment International Education website www. cambridgeinternational.org

calculate: work out from given facts, figures or information

comment: give an informed opinion

compare: identify/comment on similarities and/or differences

deduce: conclude from available information

define: give precise meaning

describe: state the points of a topic / give characteristics and main features

determine: establish an answer using the available information

explain: set out purposes or reasons / make the relationships between things evident / provide why and/or how and support with relevant evidence

give: produce an answer from a given source or recall/ memory

identify: name / select / recognise

justify: support a case with evidence / argument

predict: suggest what may happen based on available information

sketch: make a simple freehand drawing showing the key features, taking care over proportions

state: express in clear terms

suggest: apply knowledge and understanding to situations where there are a range of valid responses in order to make proposals / put forward considerations

Key words

acceleration: the rate at which the speed of an object changes

adapt: to change something

aluminium leaf: very thin aluminium foil

anomalies: results that do not fit a pattern

anomalous results: results that do not fit a pattern

approximate: a value that is close to the true value

atom: the smallest unit of a material

buffered: a way to reduce the impact or force

capillary tube: a thin glass tube

C-core: soft iron core in the shape of the letter C

charge: a store of electrical energy

circumference: the distance around the outside of a circle

compass: a device with a magnetised pointer that points North

compression: an area in a longitudinal wave where particles are closer together

control variables: the variables in the investigation that might affect your results if they are not kept constant throughout

data logger: an electronic device that records information over a set period of time

decay: when an atom releases radiation

demagnetised: when an object loses its magnetism

dependent variable: the variable that is measured in an investigation

diameter: the length of a line that goes from one side of a circle to the other and passes through the centre of the circle

dispersion: separating light into the different colours it is made up of

echo: a reflected sound wave

e.m.f. (electromotive force): the voltage of a power supply that causes a current to flow

elastic: the ability of a material to return to its original shape once a force is removed

electric motor: a device that changes electrical and magnetic energy into kinetic energy

estimate: use information available to decide on a value that is appropriate

extension: the difference between the original length and the new length of a material

frequency: the number of times a wave happens in 1 second

fulcrum: the point that an object rotates about or where it is balanced

galvanometer: an ammeter that detects small changes in current, usually micro amps

generate: to create

generator: a device that generates electricity using electromagnetic induction by transforming kinetic and magnetic energy

gravitational potential energy (g.p.e.) : the energy store of an object due to its position in a gravitational field

half-life: the time it takes for the activity of a radioactive sample to halve

incident ray: a ray of light before it hits a surface (for example, the light ray that leaves a ray box)

independent variable: the variable you will change in the investigation to see its effect

infrared radiation: an electromagnetic wave that is just beyond the red end of the visible spectrum

infrared radiation: an electromagnetic wave that is just beyond the red end of the visible spectrum

infrared transmitter: a device that emits thermal energy

insulator: a material that does not allow electrons to pass through

insulator: a material that inhibits the flow of electron or the flow of thermal energy

intensity: the power of the incident ray over a certain area – brighter lights are more intense

interaction: how two things behave in relation to one another

iron yoke: a small iron bar used to create a closed iron square

isotope: an atom of an element that contains the same number of protons but differing numbers of neutrons

justification: reason why something is correct

kinetic energy (k.e.): the energy an object has because it is moving. The greater the kinetic energy of an object, the more difficult it is to bring it to rest. The stopping distances of cars are determined by their kinetic energy

lead shot: tiny balls of lead

light gate: detects the length of time a light beam is broken for, when used in conjunction with a data logger

longitudinal wave: a wave that vibrates (oscillates) parallel to the direction of energy transfer

lux: the unit of measurement for intensity

manipulate: change or rearrange something to suit your needs

mass: the amount of matter in an object

mean: the sum of numerical results divided by the number of results

meniscus: the lowest point of the top of a liquid

model: a situation that acts or behaves in a similar way to scientific principle

molecules: a group of atoms bonded together to make the smallest unit of a chemical

normal: a line that is at a 90-degree angle to another line

ohmmeter: a device used to measure the resistance of a component in a circuit

oscillate: repeated up and down, or back and forth motion of an object

oscillation: the movement of an object from its start point to its furthest point and back again to the start

parallax error: an error that can be caused when an object is not observed from eye level. It means that the value 'seen' looks different from the actual value. For example, reading the volume of a fluid in a measuring cylinder from above, or reading the speedometer in the car from the passenger's side (makes it look like the car is travelling faster than it is)

particles: small portions of matter, for example, molecules, atoms, groups of molecules

pendulum: a weight on the end of a fixed line. it swings, constantly transferring its energy between gravitational potential energy (g.p.e.) and kinetic energy (k.e.)

perpendicular: at a right angle to something

phase: a period of time or a stage in the Moon's motion

precision: the smallest division of a measuring instrument

rarefaction: an area in a longitudinal wave where particles are further apart

ray box: a light source that can provide a single beam of light or multiple beams

reflected ray: a beam of light after it hits a surface

reflector: a surface that sound bounces off

refraction: the change of direction of a ray of light due to a change in speed as the light enters a different medium

refractive index: a number that tells us how quickly light passes through a material

regulate: to help control

relative: compared to something else

relay circuit: a low-voltage circuit that is used as a safety feature to turn on a higher-voltage circuit

reliability: the method will give the same result if repeated again

resistance: opposition to current

rhythm: the regular repeated pattern of a sound

ripple tank: creates water waves that are visible and which can be manipulated so we can observe wave properties more easily

significant: a measurable difference that is not due to chance

simulation: a computer model of what happens in the real situation

solenoid: a coil of wire in the shape of a cylinder that acts as a magnet when a current flows through it

speed: how quickly an object travels over a specific distance

stability: tendency of an object or system to stay the same

static: not moving

stationary: not moving

thermistor: a temperature-dependent resistor

time period: the time taken for one complete oscillation

transformer: a device that increases or decreases the voltage across it

transverse wave: a wave that vibrates (oscillates) at right angles to the direction of energy transfer

variable: a quantity that can change in an equation or in an experiment

vegetable black: a food colouring made of vegetable products

wavelength: the distance between two consecutive peaks, troughs or same points on the wave

weight: the force acting upon the mass of an object due to the pull of a gravitational field

work done: the amount of energy transferred from one store to another, for example, any time a force moves something in the direction in which it acts. Examples include lifting a book or an apple falling from a tree due to gravity

zero error: when a measuring device does not start at 0

Key equations

$$\text{acceleration} = \frac{\text{change in velocity}}{\text{time}}$$

$$\text{acceleration of free fall} = g = \frac{W}{m}$$

$$(\%)\ \text{efficiency} = \frac{(\text{useful energy output})}{(\text{total energy input})}\ (\times 100\%)$$

$$(\%)\ \text{efficiency} = \frac{(\text{useful power output})}{(\text{total power input})}\ (\times 100\%)$$

$$\text{kinetic energy, } E_\text{k} = \frac{1}{2}mv^2$$

$$\text{increase in gravitational potential energy, } \Delta E_\text{p} = mg\Delta h$$

$$\text{moment} = \text{force} \times \text{perpendicular distance from the pivot}$$

$$\text{momentum, } p = mv$$

$$\text{pressure, } p = \frac{F}{A}$$

$$\text{resistance, } R = \frac{V}{I}$$

$$\text{refractive index, } n = \frac{\sin i}{\sin r}$$

$$\text{specific heat capacity} = \frac{\text{energy required}}{\text{mass} \times \text{change in temperature}}$$

$$\text{specific heat capacity, } c = \frac{\Delta E}{m\Delta\theta}$$

$$\text{power, } P = \frac{\Delta E}{t}$$

average speed = $\dfrac{\text{total distance travelled}}{\text{total time taken}}$

weight = mass $\times$ g

spring constant, $k = \dfrac{F}{x}$

work done, W = force $\times$ distance moved = $Fd = \Delta E$